HEMINGWAY

THE OLD MAN AND THE SEA

NOTES

COLES EDITORIAL BOARD

ABOUT COLES NOTES

COLES NOTES have been an indispensible aid to students on five continents since 1948.

COLES NOTES are available for a wide range of individual literary works. Clear, concise explanations and insights are provided along with interesting interpretations and evaluations.

Proper use of COLES NOTES will allow the student to pay greater attention to lectures and spend less time taking notes. This will result in a broader understanding of the work being studied and will free the student for increased participation in discussions.

COLES NOTES are an invaluable aid for review and exam preparation as well as an invitation to explore different interpretive paths.

COLES NOTES are written by experts in their fields. It should be noted that any literary judgement expressed herein is just that — the judgement of one school of thought. Interpretations that diverge from, or totally disagree with any criticism may be equally valid.

COLES NOTES are designed to supplement the text and are not intended as a substitute for reading the text itself. Use of the NOTES will serve not only to clarify the work being studied, but should enhance the reader's enjoyment of the topic.

ISBN 0-7740-3338-X

© COPYRIGHT 1989 AND PUBLISHED BY
COLES PUBLISHING COMPANY LIMITED
TORONTO—CANADA
PRINTED IN CANADA

Manufactured by Webcom Limited
Cover finish: Webcom's Exclusive **Duracoat**

CONTENTS

Ernest Hemingway: Life and Works

Hemingway the Man

When *The Old Man and the Sea* appeared in 1952, Ernest Hemingway had been an international literary celebrity for more than a quarter of a century. Wherever people read books—and in a good many places where people did not read at all—the very name of Hemingway was a legend. It was a name associated with war and courage, with love and violence, with beauty and death. From bullfight arenas in Spain to lumber camps in Canada, from the great capitals of Europe to semi-tropical villages in Cuba and the Florida keys, the name Hemingway signified a romance and an ideal; the matador, the soldier, the hunter, the fighter, the lover, the disillusioned realist and the doomed romanticist—it meant all of these things, and more. Ernest Hemingway, as no other author of his time (and indeed, as few American authors of any time), had become a symbol not merely of literature and books, but of a particular way of living—and dying.

However, those critics who attempt to bully readers into awe-stricken admiration, or who suggest that anything but praise of Hemingway is in some way a failure of virile imagination, do no service to Ernest Hemingway, and even less service to literature.

The Writer as Artist

Amid all the talk of Hemingway the adventurer or representative of the Lost Generation, it is too easily forgotten that he was also a careful and precise artist—a disciplined practitioner of his literary craft. Ernest Hemingway was not less literary than were other writers; it is simply that he approached literature as a method of direct action, a method of giving form and therefore meaning to an otherwise futile and violent universe.

Just as the matador in the bullfighting arena "makes love to death" and so asserts life by surrounding both with ritual, with courage, and with will, so too does the writer act to create a dimension of truth and clarity from a nightmare vision of blind appetite or purposeless suffering. It is for good reason that Pedro, the matador in *The Sun Also Rises,* and Santiago, the fisherman in *The Old Man and the Sea,* are seen as men who are also artists—as individuals possessed of that quality of manhood essential for true living and true work. Neither Pedro nor Santiago retreats from danger or cruelty or reality. They accept it with courage; they shape it through their power of will, achieving a triumph that both demonstrates and redeems their mortality.

If Hemingway made too much of literature as a kind of "fishing for the big one;" if he saw the writer too exclusively as a sort of athlete-of-books, it is possible to say that he did so only because writing, for him, was neither a refuge nor a retreat from life, but rather

1

its confrontation. The writer, the fisherman or the bullfighter is the solitary human being who faces the blank wall of time and uses his appropriate instrument—muleta, fishing-line or typewriter—as a means of achieving the truth of form and dignity that alone give meaning to man's brief existence.

The Hemingway Aesthetic

The Hemingway type of man was even more widely known than was the Hemingway type of book, and this in itself is an indication of how completely the restless teen-ager from Oak Park, Illinois, had achieved a kind of star status unparalleled in the history of American literature. So profoundly did the legend overshadow the man, and the man overshadow his books, that it often seemed as though the books were an incidental by-product of the life of Hemingway himself.

Perhaps the books were indeed a by-product, for no man had a greater zest for life, a greater appetite for action and travel, and a greater unwillingness to be known only as a literary figure. Passivity was something he avoided throughout his career, in his work as well as in play (and for Hemingway, as for many artists, the two were closely related).

Ernest Hemingway considered life to be a kind of arena in which men used their courage, endurance and will as weapons. He considered life to be a perpetual struggle against a universe whose essential quality was one of irrational destruction, of violence without meaning. He also considered that literature was a ritual to be employed within the arena itself: a ritual of truth, precision and clarity in which a man could redeem his own inevitable defeat.

"He had destroyed his talent by not using it, by betrayals of himself . . . by laziness, sloth, and by snobbery, by pride," he says of the writer in *The Snows of Kilimanjaro,* adding that "the thought of his own death obsessed him. . . ." This was a warning that Hemingway gave to himself many times in his life, with an intense honesty characteristic of the man no less than of his work. The thought of death was far more vital for Hemingway than a mere morbidity of attitude. Death, in a basic sense, is the ultimate honesty, the final fact that cannot be falsified or cheated. Faced with the fact of his own death, a man must see his own life clearly and truly. When the writer—softened and over-protected—forgets his own identity, and is no longer capable of his previous work, he effects the attitude that he no longer cares about that work.

Success and the Artist

Hemingway was aware of the danger of celebrity—the fact that success all too often destroys the very talent that it rewards. With the laurels of success come great pressures toward smugness and laziness, and—perhaps most important—a kind of fear of risking the possibility of failure. Let the writer become too comfortable in his success, he realized, and he, like the matador who plays it safe or the fisherman who stays too close to the shore, undergoes a kind of corruption for which no displays meant to fool the public can compensate.

This would seem to be a peculiarly solemn self-reproach from a romantic adventurer. Perhaps it was not so peculiar after all, for Hemingway was, from the very beginning of his career, preoccupied with his craft, his art, his work. Even as a young man in Paris after World War I, Hemingway demonstrated a capacity for hard work, for artistic discipline, for voracious reading and calculated writing. Literature was never far from his mind, and he was occupied with far more than Parisian bar-hopping. His friends of those Parisian days make up a "who's who" of modern literature: Ezra Pound, F. Scott Fitzgerald, Ford Maddox Ford, Edmund Wilson, Gertrude Stein and many others—a long impressive list of novelists, poets and critics.

It was Gertrude Stein who once described Hemingway, despite his posture of impatience with bookish pursuits, as being a man of museums, and this description hardly fits the popular portrait of Hemingway the adventurer. In Paris, Hemingway was later to remember, he was trying to write, and found that his greatest difficulty was to note what really happened in action, what the actual things were that produced the emotion that one experienced. He was trying to learn to write, commencing with the simplest things.

Hemingway's statement is a capsule definition of what he and other writers in the United States and abroad were trying to achieve during the post-World War I period: that is, an end to literary rhetoric, and a leaner, more objective, more concrete language that would not so much talk about emotion, as recreate it. The "objective correlative" of T. S. Eliot, for example, has much in common with Hemingway's cinematic prose—a detached, carefully accurate use of language as camera, so that the reader would not be told about a particular value of emotion, but would see the exact sequence of fact, object and action that created the emotion itself.

The Distrust of Rhetoric

Hemingway's distrust of literary rhetoric was shaped by his distrust of all abstractions that would substitute slogans for experience. The non-reality of verbalized patriotism, bravery, love, sacrifice or nobility had been exposed, in the mass machinery of technological warfare, as a kind of sentimentality that falsified what it would not endure, and profited from what it piously mourned. Hemingway, and other writers of his time, insisted that phrase-mongering was the occupation of the politician or professional patriot; it was not the instrument of the writer. The literary artist would not use words for obscuring the reality of experience, but would use them as precisely and as economically as possible. Young writers had seen all the sacred

3

abstractions and fine-sounding phrases of political, religious, literary and military leaders end in the dung-heap of World War I. They demanded not more words, but fewer—words whose meaning would be clear and unmistakable, directed toward discovering experience and truth rather than avoiding them.

The fact remains, however, that not every experience has a meaning that is uniformly clear, or a truth that is uniformly simple. Experience may evoke ambiguous implications, and truth may be complex. It is one thing for a writer to render complex experiences accurately, but quite another for him to insist that an experience must be uncomplicated in order to be valid. Hemingway's own refusal to deal with areas of complex reality rather than simple action produces a certain limitation in his work. There is more to life than endurance, and there is more to dying than being killed.

Perhaps one might also say that there is more to growing old than the attempt to recapture the powers of youth—a fact that Hemingway seemed to find difficult to accept in his own lifetime, and which renders Santiago, in *The Old Man and the Sea,* in some ways pathetic rather than noble.

Limitations

That Hemingway's work has limitations is obvious enough, and it is unfortunate that efforts to explain these limitations have often aroused passions that have nothing to do with the work itself. Something of a Hemingway cult has arisen, which is encouraged by men who often seem more like cheerleaders than literary critics. Hemingway himself, of course, was partially responsible for this development. Haunted by fear of failure all his life (failure of art, failure of nerve, failure of other more intimate areas of existence), Hemingway could tolerate little criticism.

Too often, he reacted to challenges with either denunciation or sulking, and questioned the motives, not to mention the manhood, of those who actually cared enough about his work to read it instead of merely praising it. His use of baseball-boxing-hunting jargon in the most absurd circumstances indicated that Hemingway had come to believe in his own colorful public image. "I trained hard and I beat Mr. de Maupassant," he bragged to Lillian Ross of the *New Yorker*; "I've fought two draws with Mr. Stendhal and I think I had an edge on the last one." Only Hemingway could have said it, and only Hemingway could have believed it.

It is always difficult, of course, to know when a writer's subject becomes an obsession, but Hemingway's insistence, and re-insistence, on virility and manhood do have their ludicrous aspects. One cannot escape the conclusion that his perpetual assertion had its basis in some deep-rooted feelings of anxiety. The Hemingway hero is too often either unaware of—or a refugee from—what is ultimately the most dangerous area of existence: the complexities of the human soul.

Action itself, after all, may be a drug, a way of making it unnecessary to confront any experience that cannot be handled as one handles a gun or fishing line. It is possible for a man to be so frightened of life that he feels compelled to kill something; to have so little feeling for life that his entire nature is directed toward endurance and the assertion of will; and to have so little understanding of life that he uses ritual as a substitute for reality rather than as a means of shaping it.

Flight from Complexity

Throughout Hemingway's work there is a certain flight from all complexity. So often do Hemingway's heroes remind themselves not to think that we have no choice but to believe that they really mean it. It is true that Hemingway placed his heroes in situations in which thinking is not necessary—situations in which will and endurance become the primary human values. What such placing indicates, however, is the fact that Hemingway arranged his "stage-sets" very carefully. He simply refused to deal with any aspect of real life—or even real struggle—that called for a wider stock of spiritual and intellectual weapons than those at the disposal of his protagonists, or of Hemingway himself.

This reservation applies to his language as well. It may be true that, as Hemingway said, good prose is like an iceberg, with only a small part showing on the surface. But it is also true that icebergs must remain in chill and arctic waters—or they melt. If the hard surface of Hemingway's prose is in some ways admirable, in other ways it is the product of weakness rather than of strength.

This is not to say that Hemingway's work is to be dismissed as insignificant. Indeed, it was precisely because Ernest Hemingway was an artist that he could turn his own failures, his own fears, into an art that is both significant and true. In order to understand what he did produce, it is necessary to have some idea of what he could not produce. Hemingway made the best possible use of his limitations, but we must recognize those limitations in order to appreciate the use to which he put them.

Basic Elements

Three elements in Hemingway's life shaped many of his attitudes, and indeed shaped much of his work: the fact that in World War I he suffered a painful and terrible mortar wound, which made him conscious of the dread possibility of the loss of manhood; the fact that his father committed suicide; and the fact of his growing old—and the fears created by old age itself. Similar to Frederick Henry in *A Farewell to Arms,* Jake Barnes in *The Sun Also Rises,* and Santiago in

The Old Man and the Sea, Hemingway was afflicted with the fear of letting go and with the fear of thinking. The nightmare of chaos, of passivity—loss of will, loss of initiative, loss of the masculine role—was a terrible nightmare, and one to be avoided at all costs. That Hemingway evolved his own solutions to this nightmare, and based his art upon them, is something for which everyone interested in books and people must be thankful. We need not assume that the solutions were universal ones, nor need we shrink from examining the art itself.

Initiative as Value

Even in matters of love, the problem of initiative remains all-important. The woman is good only when she is passive (leaving initiative to the male) and bad when, for any reason, she takes the initiative and reduces the male to passivity. Hence, Catherine, in *A Farewell to Arms,* is indeed (as Rinaldi suggests) a sacred object, and Maria, in *For Whom the Bell Tolls,* is a provider of passion; both are good because they never take the initiative, thus forcing a man into a passive role. Bret Ashley, on the other hand, and Frances as well, in *The Sun Also Rises,* are bad because they usurp the masculine role—the former because of ironic fate (Jake Barnes' war-inflicted impotence), and the latter because of willful choice.

World War I—The Great Crusade

Very few people, least of all the volunteers themselves, understood that World War I was to be the first great war of the machine, the first war in which mechanics were far more important than heroes, and the first war in which unprecedented masses of men slaughtered each other with little or none of the glory or tests of manhood that were supposed to be part of the military experience. Military leadership had not kept pace with technological advances, and few generals had any clear idea of how to control either the machines or the masses of men at their disposal. The result was a war in which individuals were reduced to the level of helpless targets; a war in which the brave soldier and the cowardly soldier crawled about from one bloody hole to another and were likely to be killed—or not killed— quite by accident.

As a young boy in the Michigan north woods, deeply influenced by the examples and the philosophy of his father, Hemingway had learned to respect the strength and power of the individual creature alone with his own death. He had learned to respect courage and control, the right way of doing things, whether fishing for trout or killing game, and had gone to war at the age of nineteen expecting an exercise in manhood—an exercise in which the right way would be transferred to an orderly pattern of military form. What he encountered seemed to be a ridiculous joke, except that there was nothing funny about it.

As Hemingway and other young men of his generation were to

discover, the real political reason for the war had little to do with the patriotic rhetoric and noble sentiments for which the newspapers and pulpits of America were responsible. Even as a personal test of courage, the new kind of warfare was usually meaningless. Certainly it is true that for Ernest Hemingway the shock of mechanized and impersonal warfare was even greater than the shock of political corruption.

The tragic absurdity of the war was compounded by the fact that severe courts-martial were too often a desperate resource of military leaders who had no idea of how to control the vast blood bath threatening to render obsolete all their neatly drawn maps and efficiently planned campaigns. The high commands remained tragically unaware of the social revolution that had led to the creation of civilian armies. Their attempts to apply methods of discipline appropriate to professional soldiers (who had traditionally been drawn from the lowest elements of the population) created chaos when used for the new armies of World War I.

The generals had very little notion of how to use their troops efficiently, and they tended to mistreat them. Soldiers were there to die; that was their function. When any plan miscarried, when any offensive or retreat failed to take place according to schedule (the Caporetto retreat in *A Farewell to Arms,* for example), those soldiers who survived were, by that very fact, suspect. Hence, Celine, the French novelist, remarks that the military administrations "began to shoot troopers by squads, so as to improve their morale."

A New Generation

Having cast away the rose-colored spectacles of the older generation, young writers (including the young Ernest Hemingway) could look at the world around them with a fresh sense of truth. A world of moral and aesthetic values had been reduced to shambles in the conflagration of World War I. But fire cleanses as well as destroys, and after the war young writers felt that they could—indeed, that they must—discover new values based not upon sentiment, but upon reality.

These values, of course, were widely divergent, whether in art, politics or literature. The young experimenters had one thing in common: they insisted that all values had to be based on truth. They wanted no more propaganda, no more inflated talk about home, mother and country. They were less interested in saving the world than in finding out what it is, or could be. And they rejected any solution that was not based on the facts. Since the truth about life was harsh, the solution, whatever it was, would have to cope with this harshness rather than ignore it. And if all solutions were false, if—given the nature of the world— they failed to work, the only answer would be to have no solution at all.

7

The Hemingway Code

In such a case, a man would simply face up to reality with endurance, pride, courage and silence. Faced with futility, he would accept it. He would neither mouth sentimentalities nor invent lies to give meaning to a meaningless universe. He would endure. He would fashion a ritual of action that would exist by and for itself. He would create his own reality by imposing form upon chaos, and do this not only in work, but in talk and in play. There would be a code for men and women in the very words they used, in the way they hunted, drank wine, made love, knew pleasure or suffered pain. In short, the individual—in the words of Jake Barnes of *The Sun Also Rises*—would act well rather than act badly, and in so doing would triumph over futility.

Such is the Hemingway code, which was to be a major element in all his books, and a sort of final resource for all his protagonists, from Jake Barnes in *The Sun Also Rises* (a war veteran rendered physically impotent by the absurd terrors of mechanized warfare), to Santiago in *The Old Man and the Sea* (an old fisherman rendered physically weak by age and isolation). Neither Jake nor Santiago, despite their respective weaknesses, suffers loss of manhood. This is a vital aspect of the Hemingway code, for manhood is a spiritual rather than a mere physical matter. Because they will their own endurance, pride and courage, Jake and Santiago emerge strong within their manhood, unlike those individuals who, despite an appearance of power, are less than men because of their lack of individual personalities.

While futility can be opposed by means of the code, it can never be wholly defeated. Realization of this fact is what separates the men from the boys in the world of Jake Barnes, and of Santiago—Hemingway as well. The good and brave go down into dust, into failure, no less inevitably than do the bad and cowardly; there is no magic formula that will deliver us from the *nada* (nothingness) that awaits us all. There is no ticket to a Palace of Perfect Bliss that will not prove to be in reality a ticket to nowhere at all. "All is vanity," says the voice of the Old Testament *Ecclesiastes*; and it was with deliberate calculation that Hemingway set the tone for his first literary success with a flyleaf quotation from this most profoundly skeptical of all biblical books.

Fear of Old Age

From the jumble of hopes for continued youth, and fears of age, however, one element emerges as perhaps the greatest fear of all, a fear that had been close to Hemingway from the crisis of his World War I experience: that is, the fear of passivity, the nightmare (a recurrent nightmare for Ernest Hemingway) in which the individual is deprived of his manhood by becoming an object rather than originator of action. Whether sitting on a park bench and waiting for death, or growing senile in an easy chair, or whining and complaining in a hospital bed, the overriding fear is not loss of life ("it isn't hard to die," said Hemingway) but loss of initiative and will, the failure of manhood.

The problem, in short, was not how to avoid becoming an old man, but how to avoid losing one's manhood to age. Whether Hemingway ever achieved a satisfactory solution to this dilemma is not for us to judge, although the circumstances of his death would indicate that he could not and would not accept a final weakening of those powers that were so important to the protagonists of his stories.

Biographical Sketch—Early Years

Dr. Clarence E. Hemingway was a physician in Oak Park, Illinois. He was also an enthusiastic outdoorsman and a very domesticated (perhaps over-domesticated) husband to Grace Hall Hemingway, a religious and pious woman. The Hemingways had six children, and Clarence never failed in his duties as head of the family. He was a good provider, a sentimental husband and an affectionate father. In short, he was a solid and well-trained citizen who somehow felt it necessary to escape from the domestic hearth at every opportunity, using the "Great Outdoors" as a means of asserting whatever element of manhood or independence he felt was lacking in his family-directed (and perhaps woman-directed) home.

This conflict in his father—the conflict between the independent, masculine world of the outdoors, of hunting and fishing and physical endurance, as contrasted with the over-domesticated and somehow less manly town life—was later to be remembered by Ernest Hemingway, for whom the mountains were always to be a symbol of masculine clarity and purity, while the plains, or the city, were to remain a symbol of feminine complexity and danger.

Young Ernest, the second of the Hemingway children (born July 21, 1898), was profoundly influenced by his father. Despite the efforts of Grace Hemingway to raise her son with a genteel education (she had ambitions to provide Ernest with a musical education), he followed the example of Clarence, and made it clear that the only instruments he valued were fishing rods and guns: well cared for, religiously used and almost ritualistically maintained.

The typewriter, too, was to become an instrument for the young Ernest Hemingway. Although he was never a very popular boy at school, he quickly demonstrated his ability to write accurately and well, and became the editor of his school paper. That he got the job was a tribute to his skill rather than his social success, for either through choice or nature (and perhaps a combination of both) he was never a member of the select social crowd. Indeed, his school experience was often lonely and not always pleasant, but it did provide one lesson that Hemingway was never to forget: life is a hard contest which only the tough-minded are likely to survive.

Certain aspects of Hemingway's life at this time reflected his growing restlessness. He was determined, for example, to learn boxing, but was by no means a natural fighter. He achieved some mastery of boxing only at the cost of a broken nose and a serious eye injury. He actually ran away from home twice during his school years, and spent months "on the road" working at a variety of temporary and often laborious jobs.

The World War I Adventure

Like so many young men of the American Midwest, Ernest Hemingway was bored and waiting . . . waiting for some chance for adventure, for "winning his spurs" in a situation that would combine glory with danger. The European war seemed to offer just such a chance, and when America entered The Great Crusade in 1917, Hemingway promptly tried to enlist. His eye injury, however, kept him out of the service, and he had to settle for a job as cub reporter on the Kansas City *Star*. It became impossible for Hemingway to remain in Kansas City while thousands of other Americans were going off to earn their "red badges of courage" in battle and to seek adventure. He volunteered to serve as an ambulance driver on the Italian front, and left this country with high expectations. If he could not be a soldier, he would nevertheless taste the bitter glory of war.

It was a very brief taste indeed, and far more bitter than glorious. Only a few weeks after arriving in the combat zone, Ernest Hemingway was hit by a stray shell, receiving a serious wound that was to leave scars on his mind and spirit, as well as on his body. It was, in many ways, an absurd wound, and one that had very little to do with soldiering at all. At the time he was hit he had been engaged in an activity that (under the circumstances) was rather frivolous: he had been wounded while handing out chocolates to Italian soldiers.

According to Hemingway's own testimony, he was never to forget the impact of that experience. It was not so much the pain that he remembered, as the manner in which the pain was inflicted—a helpless, passive receiving of a blow from an invisible "fist" of machinery and death. Indeed, it was the passivity rather than the pain that was to remain a nightmare for Hemingway throughout his career.

A situation in which a man could be flung on his back, to receive rather than give a decisive blow, threatened far more than life; it threatened manhood itself. In a very real sense Hemingway's life and his work were to be devoted to finding and exploring those areas of existence in which men could take the initiative from pain and death by surrounding it with form, with ritual and with willed endurance. There is, in short, an essential line of causation from Hemingway's traumatic experience during World War I to his subsequent preoccupation with the masculine role. In the fishing boat, a man (Santiago in *The Old*

Man and the Sea) could be alone with his pain, his own endurance and his own will and the same is true of the bullfight arena or the hunt.

Post-World War I Days

During his post-World War I days in Paris, Hemingway was formulating the aesthetic basis of his own work, while immersing himself deeply in the work of other writers, writers of the past as well as of the present. From Mark Twain to Henry James, from the English metaphysical poet, John Donne (who wrote in the seventeenth century), to the Russian writer, Turgenev (who wrote in the nineteenth), artists of a vast variety of ages and cultures were grist for the young Hemingway's literary mill. The flyleaf quotations in his novels, which range from Donne to the *Book of Ecclesiastes,* have an oddly literary tone for a writer so often praised—and often caricatured in the praise itself—as a sort of Huckleberry Finn with a beard.

If his wound left vitally important scars on Hemingway's spirit, and if it brought his search for military glory to a violent and sudden end, it also seemed to sharpen his determination to live life as fully as he could, and to shape it according to his own talent and will. After returning to the United States, Hemingway moved to Toronto, Canada, and became a writer for the Toronto *Star* and *Star Weekly,* and found himself involved with many literary people, the most important of whom was Sherwood Anderson. He was anxious to return to Europe, and after his marriage to Hadley Richardson in 1921, left North America once again.

Hemingway as Journalist

This time he travelled widely throughout the Continent, getting to know and love Spain, Switzerland, Austria and France. Meanwhile, he continued his work as a journalist, and enjoyed a rather sensational career in this respect. At the age of twenty-three, he covered the Greek-Turkish war, and by the time he was twenty-five, he had interviewed such world-famous figures as Lloyd George, Clemençeau, and Mussolini.

After covering this war, Hemingway went to Paris and met Gertrude Stein, the *grande dame* of American writers abroad. He was seriously trying to write at this time, but all was not going well with his marriage; Hadley was pregnant and wanted to return home. For Ernest Hemingway, however, Paris was home, and nothing—not even his wife and impending family—was more important than his literary work.

His stories had begun appearing in *avant-garde* and popular magazines (including *Atlantic Monthly*), and in 1923, he published *Three Stories and Ten Poems.* In 1924, *In Our Time,* a series of thirty-two fragments, was published in Paris. The collection of Nick Adams stories was published under the same title in the United States the following year, and *The Torrents of Spring* appeared in 1926. The literary career of Ernest Hemingway was launched at last, and nothing would be allowed to stop it.

Fame and Fortune

It was not until *The Sun Also Rises* appeared in late 1926, however, that Ernest Hemingway's name became known to millions of readers. With this novel the very phrase "The Lost Generation" became a capsule description for the disillusioned young people who had seen an entire world of ethical, moral and political values shattered in the chaotic butchery of World War I. "The Lost Generation," however (a phrase coined by Gertrude Stein in a remark to Hemingway himself), was in many ways a misleading label for the young writers and critics who came out of World War I convinced of the hypocrisy and shallowness of Western civilization. If such young people distrusted the sacred cows and sacred causes of their elders, it is also true that they did not sit back and sulk over their own disillusion. An end to illusion, after all, is in itself not a bad thing and may actually be a stimulus rather than a depressant.

The Sun Also Rises made Hemingway the spokesman for the war generation. Its profound insistence upon the futility of abstract rhetoric, and its equally profound insistence that only a code of manners and action could combat this futility, captured the imagination of an age. Hemingway's personal life, however, was chaotic despite his literary success. A divorce ended his marriage to Hadley in 1927, and Hemingway—who never remained unmarried for long—wed Pauline Pfeiffer, an editor of *Vogue*, the same year. In 1928, Hemingway suffered an emotional shock rivalled only by the initial impact of the war: the death of his father, by a self-inflicted gunshot wound, under circumstances that were to be tragically repeated in the death of Ernest Hemingway himself.

Late in 1928, Hemingway left Europe and took up residence at Key West, Florida, where Patrick Hemingway was born in 1929, and Gregory, in 1932. His second major work, *A Farewell to Arms,* had appeared in 1929. The book was an immediate critical and financial success, earning the praise of readers everywhere and selling 80,000 copies in four months.

Hemingway as "Papa"

There is no doubt that Hemingway enjoyed his fame and fortune. He was far too fond of the good things of life ever to be shy about accepting the rewards of literary celebrity. The man who liked to call himself "Papa" and "The Champ" was hardly a paragon of personal modesty, and his exploits in Third Avenue bars, no less than on African safaris, were the delight of popular journalists. So determinedly did Hemingway pursue his own colorful image, that he sometimes seemed to parody himself. The profile written by Lillian Ross for the *New Yorker* magazine is a delightful account of the author's personal absurdities and of his charm.

It was not enough, however, for Ernest Hemingway to be a celebrity. He was a writer, and the job of the writer is to write. Behind all the public clowning and posturing, apart from his various roles as soldier of fortune or grizzled old warrior, Hemingway remained true to the part of his being that was neither public nor posture: the part of himself that, alone in the arena, had to carve out a ritual of meaning from blankness.

Living in Key West after the appearance of *A Farewell to Arms,* and rapidly outgrowing his physical youth, Hemingway began moving from the role of "Champ" to the role of "Papa"—a posture (and a name) he was to enjoy throughout the remainder of his career. Possessed of great financial security as a result of his two best-selling novels, the acknowledged leader of an entire literary generation, the father of three sons (John Hemingway was the son of his first marriage), Ernest Hemingway was free to write, to fish, to hunt and to travel—a freedom that he utilized with characteristic enthusiasm. In 1932, *Death in the Afternoon* appeared, and in 1933, *Winner Take Nothing* was published. During 1933, Hemingway also published the first of thirty-one articles and stories that were to appear in *Esquire* regularly for the next six years.

Hemingway and the Spanish Civil War

Hemingway, of course, was not one to stay in one place for long, not even in his lovely Key West home. He travelled extensively, especially in Africa, and one result of his journeying was *The Green Hills of Africa,* which appeared in 1935. With the outbreak of the Spanish Civil War in 1936, Hemingway entered the arena of international politics. How much of Hemingway's motivations were actually ideological or political is open to speculation, but one thing is certain: the war in Spain was a political as well as a military battleground. Hemingway had to choose his side in ideological terms if he was to justify his interest in this war.

He devoted himself to the cause of the Loyalists, or anti-Fascists, and in 1937 served in Spain as a correspondent for the North American Newspaper Alliance—service that was to solidify his hatred of the Fascist war machine, but that also resulted in considerable disillusion with the cause of the Loyalists as well. The war had revealed itself to be not simply a matter of virtue against vice, nor of saving the Spanish people and land that Hemingway loved so deeply, but rather had shown itself to be a complex and murky swamp of political ambiguities, of intellectual cross purposes, of propaganda and cruelty and expediency that too often appeared unrelated to any noble cause whatsover.

Meanwhile, Hemingway was making an attempt to assert social, rather than individual, values and responsibilities. In 1937, with *To Have and Have Not* (three related stories, two of which had been published separately), Hemingway took the position that a man cannot stand alone, that he must have a cause beyond himself for which he can fight and die. Once again, it can be debated whether Hemingway was truly interested in any cause *per se*, or whether his imagination responded to "Cause" only as a means to justify what had always been his chief theme and preoccupation, the fighting and the dying itself.

Hemingway and World War II

After completing *For Whom the Bell Tolls,* Hemingway once again faced a crisis in his personal life, and in 1940 he and Pauline first separated and then were divorced. He promptly married the writer, Martha Gelhorn, and in 1940 began new travels with his new wife. After visiting China, they settled in Cuba. When World War II erupted, Hemingway leaped into the fray in his own manner. After editing *Men at War* in 1942, he served as a war correspondent, accompanying American troops as they pushed the German forces back across western Europe.

Hemingway, of course, took to this new war with enthusiasm. Known as "Papa" to respectful troops, and a celebrity everywhere, he helped "liberate" the Ritz Hotel in Paris, actually posting a guard at the entrance with the notice: "Papa took good hotel. Plenty stuff in cellar." It was, however, Hemingway's last war adventure. The increasing complexity of ideological warfare and police actions against communism eliminated war itself as an aesthetic resource for Hemingway. Not until he left war and politics altogether, and launched Santiago's small boat on the open sea, did Hemingway produce another major work of fiction.

After World War II

The preoccupation of Hemingway with individual courage, will and endurance could not help but be seriously threatened in a time of political upheaval, a time that more than ever before represented the triumph of machines over men. World War II was a difficult subject for Hemingway to shape into art—especially since so much of his art had been based upon the need for self-contained action, ritualized form, precision of motion (and emotion) and—perhaps most important—the insistence on the absolute necessity of personal initiative as a prerequisite of manhood.

The war, for one thing, had been a gigantic operation in which the politician became more important than the soldier, and the mechanic became far more important than both.

As for the post-World War II era of cold war and continuing crisis, there was simply nothing in it for Hemingway to use. This aspect of Hemingway's work was clarified by Nemi D'Agostino in his article, "The Later Hemingway" (*Hemingway: A Collection of Critical Essays,* ed. Robert P. Weeks, Prentice-Hall, 1962).

Old Age as Nightmare

For Ernest Hemingway, far more than for most men, the spectre of age was a terrible ghost indeed. The very virtues upon which he had based his life and his art were virtues of the young. Even in his later years, Hemingway was delightfully boyish (or regrettably so, depending on one's point of view). The problem of age was never far from his mind nor, for that matter, from his conversation. In this connection, Lillian Ross' *New Yorker* piece on Hemingway (May 31, 1950) is of particular interest. "As you get older," said Hemingway, "it is harder to have heroes, but it is sort of necessary."

The problem, of course, is to decide what sort of heroism is possible as a man does get older, and in this respect Hemingway, in 1950, was still looking backward rather than forward, so that for him (as for Robert Cantwell in *Across the River and Into the Trees*) old age itself was still simply a matter of holding on to youthful appetites and youthful abilities as long as he could. "What I want to be when I am old is a wise old man who won't bore," he remarked to Miss Ross and while the waiter was pouring wine:

> I'd like to see all the new fighters, horses, ballets, bike-riders, dames, bullfighters, airplanes, sons of bitches, café characters, big international whores, restaurants, years of wine, newsreels, and never have to write a line about any of it. . . . Would like to make good love until I was eighty-five.

Throughout the interview, there is a note of buoyancy combined with uncertainty, of readiness for death juxtaposed with fear of aging, of awareness of the inevitable combined with an almost wistful assertion of youthful power, and—finally—a kind of subdued self-perspective in which Hemingway seems to be doubting his own verbal posture. All these clashing elements were intrinsic in Hemingway's own position, as they were in the position of his protagonist in *Across the River and Into the Trees*.

In the last decade or so of his life, Hemingway was searching for an outlook that would enable him to cope with the fact of his own age. In a basic sense, *Across the River and Into the Trees* reflected the urgency of just such a search. Hemingway's temporary but vivid solution was a change of personal role; he would dramatize what he could not avoid. "Because of his own absolute youthfulness," prophetically remarked one of his close friends, "he regards old-growing as an utter and complete tragedy . . . and he is not going to degrade himself by maturing or anything of that sort. All the same, since he has a sense of

15

costume, he will emphasize his decline in all its hopelessness by sprouting a white beard and generally acting the part of *senex*. We are going to get a lot of this inverted youth from him henceforth." (Quoted by Carlos Baer, *Hemingway and His Critics,* New York, 1961, p. 9.)

If the early Hemingway had been an almost legendary figure of youthful and virile adventure, the older Hemingway would take up the role of Grand Old Man, the battle-scarred veteran, the aging but still indomitable fighter. Hemingway "the Champ" would become "Papa" Hemingway—citizen of the world, still rough-edged and manfully poetic, but mellowed by experience and years, and come to full bloom as a connoisseur of life, bullfighters, women, fishing and war.

The Last Marriage

Hemingway had by no means retired from active working and living. Divorced from Martha in 1944, he immediately married Mary Walsh, a *Time Magazine* correspondent. *Across the River and Into the Trees* appeared, and met with much critical disapproval. Hemingway, it seemed clear, had entered too completely into the role of Grand Old Man of American literature. His style had become mannered, and his aging protagonist seemed to lack the intellectual equipment for the heavy burden of introspection with which Hemingway loaded his narrative.

The "Old Man" and the Nobel Prize

This negative critical response infuriated Hemingway. *The Old Man and the Sea,* which appeared in 1952, was seen by some readers as an attack on the critical "sharks" themselves. One might note that there was some justification for Hemingway's resentment. Any writer with his force of personality must expect to make literary enemies, and Hemingway had created perhaps more than his share of personal resentment. Too many critics, at any rate, had seemed to get a kind of satisfaction from the failure of *Across the River and Into the Trees,* and Hemingway, as usual, was not very hesitant about expressing his scorn for gentlemen who seemed so willing to serve as mourners at the burial of a literary career still very much alive.

After the publication of *The Old Man and the Sea,* Hemingway travelled once again, and in 1954 narrowly escaped death in an airplane crash. This event occurred the same year he received the Nobel Prize for literature. Hemingway's health was failing. After a period of illness, he met his death as the victim of a "self-inflicted gunshot wound" in 1961, at Ketchum, Idaho, in the rugged country he loved so well. He had been working until the end, leaving many unpublished manuscripts in the care of Mary. In 1963, there appeared his posthumous, and best-selling, memoir of Paris in the twenties: *A Moveable Feast.*

Critical Analysis of the Novel

NOTE: The novel is not divided into chapters. The sections in this summary are suggested by the editors of these Notes simply for the convenience of the reader.

PART ONE: PROLOGUE TO THE VOYAGE

Santiago, the "thin and gaunt" old man, had fished for eighty-four days without success. His former companion, a boy who had been ordered by his parents to join a luckier boat, was sad at the old man's failure, for even the sail of his boat "looked like the flag of permanent defeat."

Having made some money with the other boat, the boy offered to accompany the old man again. He had left, he explained, only because he was ordered to do so by his father, who had little faith. Santiago insisted that the boy stay with the lucky boat.

As they sat, the boy reminisced fondly about the first time they had gone fishing together. He insisted that he would obtain bait for the old man for tomorrow's fishing. The old man, whose "hope and confidence had never gone," accepted the offer reluctantly. The boy further declared that he would try to persuade his new master to work as far out as the old man, in case help was needed.

When they returned to the old man's poor shack, the boy said that he would take the cast net and obtain some bait. Santiago said that he would eat a bowl of rice while the boy was gone, although they both knew that there was no bowl of rice and that the cast net had been sold. While the boy was gone, Santiago would read about the American baseball games in yesterday's newspaper. Though the old man declared that the Yankees could not lose, the boy expressed his fears of other teams. Santiago urged him to have faith in the Yankees. As the boy left, they agreed that he should buy a share in the lottery, choosing the number eighty-five.

The boy returned with a meal and two beers given to him by Martin, the owner of the Terrace. As the old man ate, the boy thought that he must obtain clothes, a blanket and soap and a towel for him. While eating, they talked of baseball and of the players and managers who had visited Cuba. In their conversation, the boy declared that the old man was the best fisherman. Santiago disagreed, but did say that he did know many tricks and had resolve. The boy left, making the old man promise to wake him in the morning.

In sleep, the old man dreamed only of the places he had known in his youth. He dreamed of Africa, with its "long golden beaches," and of the lions which "played like young cats in the dusk."

PART TWO: THE VOYAGE BEGINS

Santiago rowed out of the harbor, hearing in the darkness only an occasional voice from other fishing boats. He also heard the trembling sound of flying fish, which he loved. However, he felt sorry for the delicate swallows, who seemed to be no match for the ocean, which, though kind and beautiful, could be cruel.

He always thought of the sea as *la mar*, and thought of her capricious moods as those proper to a woman. Some of the younger fishermen spoke of the sea as *el mar*, a masculine term which reflected their view of the sea as an adversary.

Before it was light, Santiago had his baits out and was drifting with the current. His preparations were precise. Each part of his hook was "sweet smelling and good tasting," and his lines were submerged at exactly the right depth. He would rather, he thought, be exact than lucky.

When the sun was two hours higher, he saw a man-of-war bird circling. The bird, he realized, must have discovered fish, and he rowed gently towards it. Flying fish broke the surface of the water, and Santiago concluded that they were being pursued by a dolphin. The bird would have little chance, for the flying fish were too swift and large for it, but the dolphin would be successful.

The dolphin moved out too fast and too far for the old man, but he contented himself with the thought that he might pick up a stray dolphin for bait and that his big fish might be somewhere near.

The shore was now far off, "a long green line with the blue hills behind it." Santiago observed the water leisurely, watching his straight lines contentedly and happy to see so much plankton, which was a sign of the presence of fish. With disgust, he saw a deadly Portuguese man-of-war, recalling the welts and sores its poison had inflicted on him in the past. He regarded the beauty of its iridescent bubbles as "the falsest thing in the sea," and loved to see the big sea turtles eating the poisonous fish. He had affection for the elegance and speed of the turtles, though he was contemptuous of their stupidity.

When the old man looked up, he saw that the bird was circling again. As he watched, a small tuna broke the surface. Others appeared, chasing the bait fish, which were trapped in panic between the tuna and the bird. A bite tightened the line under Santiago's foot, and he hauled a ten-pound albacore aboard. It would make, he said aloud, "a beautiful bait."

Now, he reflected, it was no time to think of baseball, but only of that for which he had been born. There might be a big fish with the school of tuna. In the hot sun, he was tempted simply to drift and to sleep, but he resolved to "fish the day well."

PART THREE: SUCCESS

At that moment, one of his lines jerked. He knew that one hundred fathoms down a marlin was eating the sardines from the hook. Twice, the fish nibbled at the bait. The third time, the fish took the bait securely, and the old man knew that he had hooked his fish. He prayed that the marlin would swallow the hook so that it would pierce his heart.

Santiago pulled on the line in order to lodge the hook firmly, but he could not move the fish, which began to pull the boat off slowly towards the north-west. Easing the tension on the line by bracing it against his back, Santiago was towed slowly and steadily by the fish. He thought that the strain would kill his prey, but four hours later the fish was still pulling the boat out to sea.

Land was no longer in sight. Santiago, the line still braced around his shoulders, "tried not to think but only to endure." All that night, the fish did not change direction. Santiago made himself a little more comfortable by squeezing a sack between his shoulders and the line. A stalemate had been reached: he could do nothing with the fish, and the fish could do nothing with him. He wished that he had the boy, Manolin, to help him.

During the night, he began to pity the great fish. He had never before hooked one that was so strong or behaved so strangely. The fish did not jump or rush suddenly; his fight had no panic in it. It had taken the bait like a male and it pulled like a male. He was reminded of the time he had hooked one of a pair of marlin. The female, feeding first, had been caught and pulled aboard. The male had stayed during his companion's struggles, leaping finally above the water, as though to see what had happened to his mate, before plunging into the depths. The experience had saddened both Manolin and himself.

The great fish and he, Santiago reflected, were united by their choice. The fish's choice had been to stay in deep water, "beyond all snares and traps and treacheries." Santiago's choice had been to go and find him "beyond all people." Now, no one could help either of them.

Some time before daylight, he decided to cut his bait lines and join them to his reserve coils. It was difficult work in the dark, and once the great fish gave a sudden lurch which pulled Santiago down and caused him to cut his face. He wondered why the fish had lurched so suddenly. Certainly, he reflected, the fish's back could not feel so bad as his own. He expressed his resolution aloud: "I'll stay with you until I am dead."

At daylight, Santiago realized that the fish was not tiring. The only favorable sign was that he seemed to be swimming less deeply, but the old man still could not increase the tension on the line. He was comforted temporarily by the presence of a small bird which perched on the line. He talked to the bird in order to take his mind off the pain in his back, which was stiffening with the strain of holding the line.

Suddenly, the great fish lurched again, and the bird flew off. Santiago was pulled down into the bow, and he cut his right hand on the rope. The fish, he concluded, was also feeling pain. Still longing for the company of the boy, he was annoyed at his own carelessness in injuring his working hand. He resolved to pay attention to his work and to keep up his strength by eating some of the tuna he had caught earlier. He prepared his food with difficulty, noticing that his left hand had suffered cramp. As he ate, he wished that he could feed the great fish. It was his brother. But he must kill it.

As he tried to work out the cramp in his left hand, Santiago looked across the sea and now understood his solitude. He thought of how some men feared being out of sight of land in a small boat. They were right to feel so in months of sudden bad weather, but in these months the weather was good. "Better weather for me than for you, fish," he observed.

Suddenly, the line slanted slowly upwards as the fish came to the surface. The old man then knew the extent of his plight. Without help and far from land, he had hooked a fish that was bigger than any he had ever seen or heard of, and his left hand was still gripped by cramp. As smoothly as it had appeared, the fish re-entered the water. The old man was thankful that it began again to pull on the line without panic, and did not undertake desperate measures for escape. Thank God, he thought, that fish are not as intelligent as the men who kill them.

At noon, his left hand was uncramped. Although not religious, he began to say his prayers. With his prayers said, he felt a little better, though he was suffering as much, and perhaps a little more.

He was determined to kill the fish, in spite of its greatness and glory, to show it "what a man can do and what a man endures." Besides, he must prove to Manolin that he was indeed a "strange old man," for the "thousand times he had proved it meant nothing."

As the afternoon wore on, Santiago felt very tired. He thought of the baseball games, and determined to be worthy of the great DiMaggio, "who does all things perfectly even with the pain of the bone spur in his heel."

As the sun set, he recalled, to give himself more confidence, the time in Casablanca that he had arm-wrestled with a great black man from Cienfuegos. The match had lasted from Sunday morning until Monday morning, causing blood to come from under the fingernails of both men. Santiago had triumphed, but afterwards he had had few matches and then no more, for he decided that "he could beat anyone if he wanted to badly enough" and "it was bad for his right hand for fishing."

As an airplane passed overhead, he wished that he could see the sea from that height. Then he would truly be able to see the purple backs and purple stripes or spots of the dolphin.

Just before dark, the small line that he had passed over the stern for food hooked a dolphin. He pulled the golden mammal into the boat and decided to gut it later in order to save the blood in the meat

Santiago perceived that the movement of the great fish had

slowed perceptibly. He felt he had gained on it. Though the pain in his back "had almost passed pain and gone into a dullness that he mistrusted," his right hand was only slightly cut, his left hand was no longer cramped and, unlike the fish, he had been able to eat.

In the darkness, he felt sorry for the great fish, though that did not lessen his determination to kill it. Yet, he thought, because of its dignity there was no one worthy of eating it.

Santiago knew that he must sleep if he was to keep a clear head, but he was reluctant to do so, in case the fish made a sudden movement. He inched his way towards the stern and gutted the dolphin he had caught. Returning to the bow, he ate the unappealing raw meat and decided to sleep.

His dreams were interrupted by the sudden jumping of the fish, whose movement pulled the old man heavily against the bow. The pulling on the line cut his left hand. In the first light before sunrise, Santiago saw that the fish had changed direction and was now heading eastwards with the current. He concluded that it was beginning to tire, and he began to wait for it to circle.

Then the great fish began to circle, thrusting now and then with its spear at the wire leader on the line. With each turn, Santiago was able to pull in more line. At last he saw the fish turn a little on its side in response to a pull on the line. Exhausted, Santiago struggled to turn the fish over. Time and again he failed. Finally, taking "all his pain and what was left of his strength and his long-gone pride," he was able to turn the fish on its side as it glided close to the boat. Quickly, the old man stood on the line, lifted his harpoon as high as he could, and drove the iron into the fish. It lurched into the air, "showing all his great length and width and all his power and his beauty," and crashed on its back into the ocean. With his head in his hands, Santiago reflected on the work he must do to bring his catch to shore.

PART FOUR: TRAGEDY IN TRIUMPH

Santiago knew that the fish was too big to bring into the boat. Therefore, he lashed it securely to the side and prepared to return to the harbor. To give himself strength, he ate small shrimps from the yellow Gulf weed that floated by, and drank half of one of the two drinks of water he still had left in his bottle.

The skiff sailed well, in spite of the attached weight. Towards the end of his battle, when he had been feeling so badly, it had all seemed like a dream. Now, by looking at the fish and at his cut hands and by the feel of his back, he knew it had truly happened.

As he sailed, his head started to become a little unclear. With the fish alongside the boat, he was not sure whether he was bringing the fish in, or whether it was bringing him in. Of one thing he was sure: "I am only better than him through trickery and he meant me no harm."

The first shark struck an hour later, attracted by the spilled blood of the fish. Feeling helpless, Santiago prepared his harpoon to battle the marauder. As the shark tore into the dead fish, the old man pierced the attacker's brain with the harpoon. The shark was killed, but not before it had torn forty pounds of meat from the great fish. Santiago felt as though he himself had been hit.

It had, he thought, been too good to last. He wished that he were at home and had never hooked the fish, but he comforted himself with the thought that "man is not made for defeat."

His own thoughts and baseball were all he had left. He knew now that his task was hopeless. When he reached the inner currents, there would be other sharks. However, he decided, it was a sin to be without hope, though he did not really understand sin. Perhaps he had committed a sin in killing the fish. Yet, it seemed to be part of his destiny and the destiny of the fish. Moreover, he had loved, and still loved, the fish. Perhaps that meant that his act was not a sin. Nevertheless, he reflected, he had enjoyed killing the shark, for he had killed it well.

After two hours, he saw two more sharks. He prepared for the coming battle by taking up an oar to which he had lashed his knife, for the shark he had killed had disappeared into the sea with his harpoon. The struggle with these sharks proved more difficult than his encounter with the first. One of them attacked from under the skiff, forcing Santiago to bring the boat around in order to reach the attacker. The old man killed both of them, but not before they had ripped away one quarter of the great fish. Everything now felt wrong, and he wished that it had all been a dream. "I shouldn't have gone out so far, fish," he observed.

There was nothing left to do but rest and try to get his bleeding hands ready for the next battle. The next attacker was a single shovel-nose. Santiago killed it, but snapped his knife in the process. His only remaining weapons were the gaff, the two oars, the tiller and a short club. He knew that the sharks had beaten him, but he decided to fight as long as he had weapons. Two more sharks appeared to attack the fish. They were successful in tearing at its flesh, and Santiago was only able to drive them off. Now, he did not want to look at the great fish, for he knew that half of it had been destroyed. He expressed his feelings aloud to the fish: "Fish that you were. I am sorry that I went out too far. I ruined us both."

Around ten o'clock at night, he saw the reflected glare of the lights of Havana. By midnight, he was fighting again, and this time the struggle was truly hopeless. Sharks appeared in a pack and left only when nothing remained of the great fish.

Santiago knew then that he was truly beaten. He settled back, without thoughts or feelings, to bring the boat to the harbor. "It is easy," he thought, "when you are beaten. I never knew how easy it was." Nothing had really beaten him, he concluded; he had simply gone out too far.

PART FIVE: EPILOGUE

When the old man sailed into the harbor, everyone was in bed. He dragged the boat on shore and shouldered the mast. With deep tiredness he began his climb home. He climbed and fell under the weight and rested until he reached his shack. Once there, he took a drink of water and threw himself down to sleep, "his arms straight out and the palms of his hands up."

Manolin came next morning before Santiago was awake and wept at the sight of the fisherman's injured hands. He left to bring coffee.

At the harbor, many fishermen were examining the remains of the old man's catch. One of them declared that it was eighteen feet long. Crying, the boy went for coffee. The proprietor of the Terrace stated that there had never been such a fish. Manolin's only concern was that they should not bother Santiago.

When Santiago awoke, the boy forbade him to sit up and gave him coffee. The old man declared he had been beaten, but Manolin hastened to point out that the fish had not beaten him. The boy began to make plans for future fishing and announced that, in spite of his family, he would sail with Santiago. As Manolin left to obtain food and newspapers, he was crying again.

That afternoon, a woman from a party of tourists stared without comprehension at the spine of the great fish, and asked a waiter what it was. "Sharks," he replied, meaning to explain what had happened. Her response was that she did not know that sharks had such handsome tails.

At the shack, Santiago slept, dreaming about lions, while the boy sat by him.

Character Sketches

The Old Man and the Sea is an unusual book for a number of reasons. To begin with, the spare style has a cadence and rhythm which is distinctly recognizable as Hemingway's. Further, the nature of the narrative itself is distinctive, for what is essentially a simple story of a fisherman confronted by a formidable adversary, the sea, becomes a tale of universal significance, in which the opponents are Man and Life. However, the book is unusual too in the characterizations which it offers. There are few characters in the novel. The old man, Santiago, is the central figure. Beyond him, only the boy, Manolin, emerges with any clarity or detail. Apart from those two, the other people in the novel stand in the shadows—vague, insubstantial figures who do not share in the dominant conflict. There is, for example, Martin, the compassionate and charitable owner of the Terrace who responds sympathetically to the boy's pleas for the old man; a fisherman, Pedrico, known only by his name and the fact that he is to get the head of the great marlin; a waiter at the Terrace; and a male and female tourist who are only idly interested in what has happened. As a result, the focus upon Manolin and, to an even greater extent, upon Santiago is of crucial importance in understanding the novel.

Santiago

On the surface, the portrait of Santiago, the old man of the title, is simple and straightforward. Santiago is a poor peasant fisherman, "thin and gaunt with deep wrinkles in the back of his neck." His body bears the marks of his trade. For example, the skin of his face bears brown blotches, caused by the burning reflection of the sun's rays upon the tropical sea. In addition, his hands reveal "deep-creased scars from handling heavy fish on the cords." Everything about him, except his eyes, testifies to his age. His poverty is equally evident. He lives in a shack made from palms and furnished with only three items of furniture—a bed, a table and a chair. At night, he rolls up his trousers to form a pillow, spreads old newspapers over the bedsprings, and covers himself with the only blanket he possesses. So poor is he that his shirt has been patched and re-patched, so that it was "like the sail and the patches were faded to many different shades by the sun." Not only is he too poor to afford a newspaper, he is too poor to buy food for himself or to purchase sardines for bait. It is little wonder, then, that the sail of his boat, "patched with flour sacks," resembled "the flag of permanent defeat." Such details, of course, arouse feelings of pathos for the old man. They enable us to enter sympathetically into his struggle, for that struggle is crucial for him. He does not fish for sport or amusement; fishing is his livelihood. Upon that work depends even the poverty-stricken existence that he leads. Furthermore, his age, too, makes the struggle a crucial one. He must engage in his desperate battle, not at the height of his physical powers, but at a time when the weaknesses of his body are acutely evident to him and at a time when physical ease and sleep are seductive attractions. However, though age and poverty are two aspects of Santiago which stimulate our sympathy for him in his experience, there is more, much more, in Santiago which is worthy of close examination. The simplicity, then, is deceptive, and the portrait is both complex and intriguing.

Suggestions of more complex significance emerge early in *The Old Man and the Sea*. They are subtly suggested by the opening words of the novel—"He was an old man who fished alone in a skiff in the Gulf Stream . . . ." There, the narrative focus is cinematic in technique. All of the details—the omission of the old man's name, the mention of fishing alone in a tiny boat, the connotations of the vastness of nature in the name of the Gulf Stream—give a picture as seen by a camera at long-distance. The focus creates the mood, in which the solitude, the smallness of man and the vastness of Nature are emphasized. Consequently, there are clues immediately that this story is, in a sense, not the story of one man and his struggle, but of Man and his struggle.

Other details emphasize in a similar fashion the universal significance of Santiago. For example, the scars on his hands are said to be "as old erosions in a fishless desert." Again, with this detail, the focus is important. When first mentioned, the scars are simply the marks left by years of handling heavy fish on the lines. With the addition of the desert simile, they become more than a detail adding to the believability of the portrait of a fisherman: they are linked with Nature and the timeless movements of its landscape. In a similar vein, the eyes of the old man suggest the epic proportions of his character. We are told that everything about the old man was old—except his eyes. His eyes are "the same color as the sea" and are "cheerful and undefeated." The first detail emphasizes once more the link between Santiago and Nature, extending further suggestions of a significance beyond the particular. The second detail adds heroic qualities to the portrait. In spite of failure, the old man is undefeated. He possesses, it is suggested, courage and resolution. These qualities are emphasized again before the old man sets out on his remarkable expedition, for we are told that "His hope and his confidence had never gone."

These suggestions of the significance of Santiago's personality are given early in the novel, and they are basic to an understanding of what follows. Yet, at that stage, they are little more than suggestions, the author's fragmentary hints of significance. The truly heroic proportions of the portrait emerge fully in the novel as a whole. These more complex aspects of Santiago are the subject of the analysis which follows.

Most obvious is Santiago's *pride in his craft*. To him, fishing is not simply a job, an unpleasant task which he must perform in order to exist. His fishing is his vocation. By his own confession, fishing is "the thing that I was born for." Thus, though a champion at arm-wrestling, he has given up this idle amusement because "it was bad for his right hand for fishing." His lot as a fisherman is a destiny he has accepted with pride, as he makes clear on his perilous journey back to the harbor with his great catch:

. . . Perhaps it was a sin to kill the fish. I suppose it was even though I did it to keep me alive and feed many people. But then everything is a sin. Do not think about sin. It is much too late for that and there are people who are paid to do it. Let them think about it. *You were born to be a fisherman as the fish was born to be a fish.* San Pedro was a fisherman as was the father of the great DiMaggio.

But he liked to think about all things that he was involved in and since there was nothing to read and he did not have a radio, he thought much and he kept on thinking about sin. You did not kill the fish only to keep alive and to sell for food, he thought. *You killed him for pride and because you are a fisherman.* . . . [Italics added]

That is not to say that Santiago is supreme at his craft. He refuses to accept Manolin's praise that he is "the best fisherman." However, significantly, he does happily accept the boy's amended judgment: "There are many good fishermen and some great ones. But there is only you." The distinction is important to an understanding of Santiago. He does possess skill and expertise. He knows many tricks. Indeed, as he thinks of the marlin he has caught, he declares, "I am only better than him through trickery. . . ." What distinguishes Santiago is his pride in the ritual of his craft. His work must be performed according to a certain form. Thus, not only is the result of his activity important, but also the manner of its accomplishment. This concept helps to explain Santiago's pride in the precise, ritualistic way in which he sets his lines:

> . . . He looked down into the water and watched the lines that went straight down into the dark of the water. He kept them straighter than anyone did, so that at each level in the darkness of the stream there would be a bait waiting at exactly where he wished it to be for any fish that swam there. Others let them drift with the current and sometimes they were at sixty fathoms when the fishermen thought they were at a hundred.
>
> But, he thought, I keep them with precision. Only I have no luck anymore. But who knows? Maybe today. Every day is a new day. It is better to be lucky. But I would rather be exact. Then when luck comes you are ready.

The precision is the expression of Santiago's integrity as a fisherman. It is a ritual to which he must adhere. It is a code of conduct which is the deepest expression of his manhood. Faced with a capricious ocean and creatures of the deep that are more powerful than he, man can only bring to bear all the resources of his intelligence and artistry. This helps to explain Santiago's preoccupation with the concept of dignity. He is impatient, for example, with the cramp in his left hand, not because it hampers him in his struggle, but because it is "unworthy of it to be cramped." Further, he admires the great marlin as an adversary. The marlin's power and endurance are not the only qualities which evoke that admiration. More important is the manner in which the marlin has fought. It proved its own worth as a creature in the way in which it performed its appointed task. It, too, had observed the ritual; it, too, had expressed the dignity of the expected code in action. From that sprang Santiago's admiration:

Then he was sorry for the great fish that had nothing to eat and his determination to kill him never relaxed in his sorrow for him. How many people will he feed, he thought. But are they worthy to eat him? No, of course not. There is no one worthy of eating him from the manner of his behavior and his great dignity.

This sense of the dignity of the ritual also illuminates Santiago's sorrow after the sharks had torn the body of the great marlin. He is not sorrowed by the loss of his catch so much as he is sorrowed by the indignity inflicted upon a once noble creature. The sharks had made "everything wrong." Such is his sorrow at the affront suffered by his former opponent that he "did not want to look at the fish," because "He knew that half of him had been destroyed." His only consolation lies in the thought of the magnificent battle the marlin might have waged with the sharks, had it been alive:

He could not talk to the fish anymore because the fish had been ruined too badly. Then something came into his head.
'Half fish,' he said. 'Fish that you were. I am sorry that I went too far out. I ruined us both. But we have killed many sharks, you and I, and ruined many others. How many did you ever kill, old fish? You do not have that spear on your head for nothing.'
He liked to think of the fish and what he could do to a shark if he were swimming free. I should have chopped the bill off to fight them with, he thought. But there was no hatchet and then there was no knife.
But if I had, and could have lashed it to an oar butt, what a weapon. Then we might have fought them together.

Precision and dignity, then, are important elements in Santiago's pride. Consequently, that pride must not be confused with empty vanity. The old man is not vain. He does not regard himself as "the best fisherman." For example, pulled helplessly by the marlin, he admits frankly his "lack of preparation." Indeed, not only does he lack vanity, but he recognizes, without self-consciousness, that he possesses humility: "He was too simple to wonder when he had attained humility. But he knew he had attained it and he knew it was not disgraceful and it carried no loss of true pride." The "true pride" in his craft is more than a recognition of his own skill; it is the expression of what he is, the expression of his manhood. He is what he is, "a strange old man," and his pride in his craft moves him to demonstrate, through his craft, his uniqueness:

. . . But I will show him what a man can do and what a man endures.

"I told the boy I was a strange old man" he said. "Now is when I must prove it."

The thousand times that he had proved it meant nothing. Now he was proving it again. Each time was a new time and he never thought about the past when he was doing it.

In the light of this concept of pride, Santiago's admiration for the baseball player, Joe DiMaggio, becomes comprehensible. In his own way, Santiago sees a bond, a kinship, between himself and DiMaggio. Just as the old man was not "the best fisherman," so DiMaggio was not the best baseball player. But he was a champion and, like the old man, took pride in his craft. He was a team player whose presence "made the difference." The old man acknowledges that Dick Sisler could hit great drives, and Manolin agrees that there was "nothing ever like them," but DiMaggio was DiMaggio, and could be counted upon to contribute all that he had to the game. So, too, the old fisherman expresses in his craft all of the qualities that make him what he is as an old man. He is not "the best"—but he *is* Santiago. Consequently, Santiago wishes to emulate DiMaggio, not in his accomplishments or his fame, but in his integrity in what he does. Thus, in his encounter with the marlin, the old man declares that he "must be worthy of the great DiMaggio who does all things perfectly even with the pain of the bone spur in his heel." Later, when he has triumphed over the marlin, his thought is that "the great DiMaggio would be proud of me today." Finally, after the first shark has struck the marlin and Santiago has killed the marauder, he is content that he has done what he could and done it well. No more could be expected. The ritual has been performed as it should be; his expertise has expressed his manhood. At that point, his thoughts turn once more to DiMaggio:

But I must think, he thought. Because it is all I have left. That and baseball. I wonder how the great DiMaggio would have liked the way I hit him in the brain? It was no great thing, he thought. Any man could do it. But do you think my hands were as great a handicap as the bone spurs?

DiMaggio, then, is an image for all the rightful pride that belongs to a man as a man. The pride is the sense of integrity and wholeness gained from doing things well and in a manner appropriate to the craft. This pride is one of the most important characteristics which distinguishes Santiago. It transforms him, so that he is not simply a poor Cuban fisherman facing adversity; he becomes all men who, with dignity and integrity, do what they must in the face of life's ironies.

A second aspect of Santiago's personality is his *compassion*. The quality of that compassion is seen almost as soon as the old man begins his voyage. As he rows in the darkness, he reflects on the birds which fly over the ocean:

> . . . He was sorry for the birds, especially the small delicate dark terns that were always flying and looking and almost never finding, and he thought, the birds have a harder life than we do except for the robber birds and the heavy strong ones. Why did they make birds so delicate and fine as those sea swallows when the ocean can be so cruel? She is kind and very beautiful. But she can be so cruel and it comes so suddenly and such birds that fly, dipping and hunting, with their small sad voices are made too delicately for the sea.

The compassion is evidently not mere emotionalism; it is not a naïve sentimentality. It is based upon a genuine sense of brotherhood, in which it is seen clearly and vividly that all creatures, both man and beast, are placed in a universe in which triumphs are won only with difficulty and in which the best one can do is to struggle with the handicaps that are an integral part of one's being. That is why Santiago is able to reflect upon the nature of the ocean without feeling hostility. The sea is what it was created to be. Its capriciousness is simply the fulfilment of its nature and is not to be resented or regarded negatively. Thus, while some of the fishermen spoke of the sea as *el mar*, with the use of the masculine article expressing their view of it as "a contestant or a place or even an enemy," Santiago always thought of the sea as *la mar*, "which is what people call her in Spanish when they love her." He is thus able to accept the sea for what she is, without bitterness or hostility:

> . . . But the old man always thought of her as feminine and as something that gave or withheld great favors, and if she did wild or wicked things it was because she could not help them. The moon affects her as it does a woman, he thought.

The universe is as it was meant to be, and all that creatures can do is to fulfil their ordained function. At its best, this realization results in a compassionate sense of brotherhood, seen very clearly in the old man's talk to a small bird which visits his skiff:

> A small bird came towards the skiff from the north. He was a warbler and flying very low over the water. The old man could see that he was very tired.
> The bird made the stern of the boat and rested there. Then he flew around the old man's head and rested on the

where he was more comfortable. "How old are you?" the old man asked the bird. "Is this your first trip?"

The bird looked at him when he spoke. He was too tired even to examine the line and he teetered on it as his delicate feet gripped it fast.

"It's steady," the old man told him. "It's too steady. You shouldn't be that tired after a windless night. What are birds coming to?"

The hawks, he thought, that come out to sea to meet them. But he said nothing of this to the bird who could not understand him anyway and who would learn about the hawks soon enough.

"Take a good rest, small bird," he said. "Then go in and take your chance like any man or bird or fish."

It encouraged him to talk because his back had stiffened in the night and it hurt truly now.

"Stay at my house if you like, bird," he said. "I am sorry that I cannot hoist the sail and take you in with the small breeze that is rising. But I am with a friend."

Here, Santiago accepts the small bird as part of the universe, viewing its struggle for survival as being no less significant than his own. Man, bird and fish are alike in having to take their chances. Hence, there is no scorn for the bird in its fragility, nor is there unfeeling indifference. Santiago and the bird are part of the brotherhood of all creation, and the fisherman accepts that bond with naturalness, kindness and grace.

That same compassionate sense of brotherhood dominates Santiago's relationship with the great marlin which he pursues. As he remarks to the small bird, in his contest with the marlin he feels that he is "with a friend." That does not mean that he can forsake his stalking of the fish. Both must fulfil their destiny. The fisherman must pursue and the fish must evade his pursuer. Santiago will kill the marlin, but that does not diminish his love or his respect for it: "Fish," he said, "I love you and respect you very much. But I will kill you dead before this day ends." This love and respect is evident throughout the hunt, and the bond between the hunter and the hunted, between the fisherman and the fish, is remarkable and moving. For this reason, Santiago sees them as being united in their suffering: "You're feeling it now, fish," he said. "And so, God knows, am I." Later, when the first shark tears forty pounds of flesh from the marlin, Santiago deeply feels the outrage visited upon his fish: "it. . . was as though he himself were hit." When the incident is over, the fisherman reaches over the side of the skiff, cuts a piece of meat from the marlin and eats it. The act is not without meaning, for it expresses in the deepest possible way his communion with the fish. They are one, just as Jesus of Nazareth expressed his oneness with his disciples by offering them, before his death, bread and wine as the symbols of his body and his blood.

In part, this compassionate feeling of the unity of all creatures is an expression of Santiago's *reverence*. He is not, in a formal sense, a religious man. The religious pictures in his shack are "relics of his wife." He is forthright in his statement of the truth: "I am not religious." When Santiago mentions God, as he does frequently, the references are little more than uses of the name: "Thank God he is travelling and not going down;" "God let him jump;" "You're feeling it now, fish," he said. "And so, God knows, am I;" "If sharks come, God pity him and me;" "But God knows he has had enough chances to learn;" "God knows how much that last one took." His attitude towards formal religion is best understood in a passage which occurs in the midst of his trial:

> "I am not religious," he said. "But I will say ten Our Fathers and ten Hail Marys that I should catch this fish, and I promise to make a pilgrimage to the Virgin of Cobre if I catch him. That is a promise."
>
> He commenced to say his prayers mechanically. Sometimes he would be so tired that he could not remember the prayer and then he would say them fast so that they would come automatically. Hail Marys are easier to say than Our Fathers, he thought.
>
> "Hail Mary full of Grace the Lord is with thee. Blessed art thou among women and blessed is the fruit of thy womb, Jesus. Holy Mary, Mother of God, pray for us sinners now and at the hour of our death. Amen." Then he added, "Blessed Virgin, pray for the death of this fish. Wonderful though he is."
>
> With his prayers said, and feeling much better, but suffering exactly as much, and perhaps a little more, he leaned against the wood of the bow and began, mechanically, to work the fingers of his left hand.

The attitude illustrated here is assuredly not that of a man who is religious in a formal sense. The prayers are said "mechanically" and quickly, "so that they would come automatically." Further, in the midst of his religious feeling, Santiago does not lose sight of the practical. He finds Hail Marys easier to say than Our Fathers. When his prayers are finished, he recognizes his situation as being unchanged; he is suffering "exactly as much, and perhaps a little more." At the close of the incident, he does not omit practical activity, for he begins to work the fingers of his left hand. Moreover, the bargain he makes with God, should he get the fish, is no more than a conventional response to acute need; it does not necessarily denote any special kind of religious feeling. Thus, while Santiago certainly does not deny God, equally certainly, he cannot be regarded as pious in an orthodox fashion.

For this reason, "reverence" has been chosen as the word which might best describe his response to the universe. In fact, his attitude is, startlingly, reminiscent of the attitude of Jesus of Nazareth in some respects. There is, of course, a large measure of difference between the two. To Santiago, God seems to be little more than a name, whereas to Jesus, God was Father. In addition, to Jesus, man's paramount duty was to the service of God, whereas Santiago seems to view his duty as a commitment to the true expression of his own being. However, in their response to the life around them, Santiago and Jesus of Nazareth would seem to be like spirits. Both expressed a deep reverence for life. With both Jesus and Santiago, that reverence expresses itself most often in the word 'love'. Thus, Santiago loves the ocean, in spite of its moods. To Santiago, the sea is *la mar,* "which is what people call her in Spanish when they love her." His thoughts of the turtles reflect the same love:

> He had no mysticism about turtles although he had gone in turtle boats for many years. He was sorry for them all, even the great trunk-backs that were as long as the skiff and weighed a ton. Most people are heartless about turtles because a turtle's heart will beat for hours after he has been cut up and butchered. But the old man thought, I have such a heart too and my feet and hands are like theirs.

In a similar vein, he regards the great marlin as a brother, and not as an enemy. Even his love for Manolin is deepened by the contest he endures. After the first shark has made its assault upon the marlin, Santiago's thoughts turn once more to the boy: "The boy keeps me alive, he thought. I must not deceive myself too much." The love which Santiago feels is actually the same love of which Coleridge's ancient mariner learned only after an experience in which he came close to death. Coleridge's mariner expressed his lesson simply:

> He prayeth well, who loveth well
> Both man and bird and beast.

When the mariner began his fateful voyage, this wisdom was not part of his experience. He revealed his egotism in the thoughtless, senseless and unjustified act of killing the harmless albatross which followed their ship. As a man, he had asserted an arrogant supremacy which was not rightfully his. Only when he was surrounded by death, with the ship becalmed on a stagnant, tropical ocean, could he find within himself the impulse to give thanks for all life. From that experience came the wisdom of love. In contrast, Santiago embodies the wisdom of love from the beginning. That love dominated his hunt of the marlin, a hunt that was undertaken with a reverential respect for the pursued creature. The same reverence is evident in all aspects of the old man's life—in his attitude towards his craft, in his respect for the great DiMaggio, and in his communion with the other creatures he encounters on his voyage.

Santiago is a memorable figure, possessing admirable qualities. He bears his poverty nobly and with dignity, even though he seems to be unaware of the irony in his advice to the young boy—". . . I try not to borrow. First you borrow. Then you beg."—and allows the young boy to provide for him. He does not lose his integrity. He is a figure the reader can trust, for he is honest and spontaneous in his responses. It is thus fitting that the only creature which disgusts him is the Portuguese man-of-war. He is sensitive to the fish's beauty as he observes its iridescent bubbles, but he knows its true nature. It is "the falsest thing in the sea." Its very nature is deceptive. That quality is obviously one which the old fisherman detests. For his own nature is whole. He is what he is, and his actions express his being. Above all, he does not want to "fail himself." He may fail in his task, but he must not fail himself as a man. With this integrity, he may be beaten and he may be destroyed, but he will not be defeated. To the last, he will express his manhood, not in a physical sense only, but also spiritually.

For this reason, other aspects of Santiago are secondary to the heroic proportions of his integrity. His simplicity, his honesty, his humility, his skill at his craft, his joy in simple pleasures, his loyalty—all of these admirable qualities serve only to highlight the central integrity of the man. That integrity is made up of pride, compassion and love. As a result, the figure which emerges has heroic proportions and his struggle becomes epic in dimensions. As Clinton S. Burhans Jr. observed, ". . . Santiago represents a noble and tragic individualism revealing what man can do in an indifferent universe which defeats him, and the love he can feel for such a universe and his humility before it."

In part, the epic quality of the portrait of Santiago finds substance in the religious imagery associated with the old man. His name is derived from the Spanish form for St. James, who was one of the twelve disciples chosen by Jesus of Nazareth. Like Santiago, James was also a fisherman, born to his calling, for his father was also a fisherman. In addition, St. James seems to have been, with Peter and John, one of the apostles who were on terms of special intimacy with Jesus. The religious connotations do not stop there, however. There are even suggestions in the portrait of Santiago of a parallel between the old man and Jesus Himself. For example, like Jesus, Santiago is a fisherman and a teacher, with Manolin as his faithful disciple. Like Jesus, the old man embodies the quality of humility. Like Jesus, he knows the pain of torn hands and a back lashed by suffering. Again, like Jesus, in the hour of his greatest suffering he feels a pain akin to that experienced when nails are driven through hands. Like Jesus, Santiago's hour of testing begins on noon of the first day and ends on noon of the third day. Santiago is further reminiscent of Jesus towards the end of the novel, when he wearily shoulders the cross-like mast and stumbles agonizingly home to his shack. Finally, as the old man flings himself upon his bed in exhaustion, he lies in a crucifixion attitude, his arms stretched out and the palms of his hands facing up. The parallels are striking.

That is not to say, of course, that there is an exact identification of Santiago with Jesus, or that the old man is meant to present the definitive portrait of a religious man. Rather, the religious parallels add to the epic dimensions of the characterization. On the one hand, the parallels underline the significance of what happens, setting the events against a background of larger, crucial meaning. On the other hand, the parallels emphasize the allegorical aspects of Santiago. He becomes more than an old fisherman gambling desperately on a grand venture. He becomes all men who, with dedication, nobility and courage, meet life frankly and steadily and impressively.

Manolin

The reader learns little of the boy, Manolin, in terms of concrete detail. We know that he has customarily been Santiago's companion in fishing. Their association began very early, when Manolin was only five years of age. In spite of the old man's months of bad luck, the bond between them has not been weakened. True, Manolin no longer sails with the old man, but the boy has not deserted his master willingly. Manolin's father, who does not share his son's faith in Santiago, has forced the boy to fish with a luckier boat. But the bond between the two is still strong and close. Thus, Manolin felt Santiago's lack of success keenly: "It made the boy sad to see the old man come in each day with his skiff empty and he always went down to help him carry either the coiled lines or the gaff and harpoon and the sail that was furled around the mast." Further, Manolin tends constantly to the old man's needs. When Santiago returns from fishing, the boy brings him a supper of stew, black beans, rice and fried bananas, which he has obtained from Martin, the owner of the Terrace. He also obtains sardines for bait. His respectful care of Santiago is plainly evident:

> Where did you wash? the boy thought. The village water supply was two streets down the road. I must have water here for him, the boy thought, and soap and a good towel. Why am I so thoughtless? I must get him another shirt and a jacket for the winter and some sort of shoes and another blanket.

His care does not weaken. When Santiago is to set out on his fateful expedition, Manolin insists that the old man should wake him in the morning, so that he can assist in carrying the fishing gear to the boat. In the end, when Santiago returns home, exhausted after his harrowing experience on the ocean, beaten once more though not defeated, the boy's regard for the old man is not diminished. He attends to Santiago's needs at once. He brings hot coffee and borrows wood for a fire. At that point, he shares enthusiastically in the fisherman's plans for the future and, typically, runs off for food, a clean shirt and the newspapers.

In his relationship with Santiago, Manolin proves himself to be a boy of unusual and striking qualities for one his age. His sensitivity, his compassion and his practical thoughtfulness are characteristics which make his personality both charming and attractive for the reader.

However, the relationship does more than simply add aspects of tenderness and selflessness to the novel. The character of Manolin makes two major contributions to the novel.

In the first place, Manolin underlines the religious imagery of *The Old Man and the Sea*. He is not simply a boy who happens to be fond of an old man and, in the unselfishness of youth, provides for his companion's needs. The relationship between the two is presented in clearly religious terms. Santiago is the master, and Manolin is his disciple. The bond between them, apart from the obvious affection, is that of teacher and student. For example, Santiago is the one who initiated the boy into the mystery of the craft of fishing. Neither word, "initiated" or "mystery," is too strong to use in this context. When Manolin recalls his first expedition with the old man, his words become almost a chant, in which the sights, sounds and smells of that first time are experienced again:

> I can remember the tail slapping and banging and the thwart breaking and the noise of the clubbing. I can remember you throwing me into the bow where the wet coiled lines were and feeling the whole boat shiver and the noise of you clubbing him like chopping a tree down and the sweet blood smell all over me.

There is more here than the picture of a boy learning the routine of a job. It is a picture of a spirit captured in its totality. Manolin speaks with the conviction and vigor of the convert. Like the convert, he has experienced his moment of joyous revelation and can re-live it at will. In that moment, he gained more than information, more than knowledge; he became a fisherman, with all that that means in relation to Santiago. Thus, when the old man asks him, "Can you really remember that or did I just tell it to you?" Manolin is able to speak from personal knowledge: "I remember everything from when we first went together." For what they share is much more than a particular skill. It is—significantly—a faith. In contrast, Manolin's father, we are told, "hasn't much faith;" he has ordered his son to fish with a luckier boat. In this regard, Manolin's insight is remarkable. He is able to share an experience that many who are older can not. This is true even of other fishermen, who are seemingly of two kinds. There are those who would appear to be familiar with fishing as a craft which involves not only skill but also a man's destiny, and those who, like Manolin's father, are insensitive to the mystery. This suggestion reveals itself when Manolin and Santiago go to the Terrace to sit with the other fishermen:

> They sat on the Terrace and many of the fishermen made fun
> of the old man and he was not angry. Others, of the older
> fishermen, looked at him and were sad. But they did not
> show it and they spoke politely about the current and the
> depths they had drifted their lines at and the steady good
> weather and of what they had seen.

The contrast between the two groups of fishermen is vivid, and seems to suggest that the more compassionate fishermen are older and—no less important—wiser. It is as though for some, fishing has brought not only initiation into a skill, but also initiation into a view of life. Like Santiago, they have become aware, perhaps, of "The heartache and the thousand natural shocks that flesh is heir to."(*Hamlet*) In pitting their resources against Nature, they have, perhaps, heard what Wordsworth described as "the still sad music of humanity." As a result, they are not prepared to mock another's misfortune; their awareness of life's ups and downs prevents such behavior. Remarkably, Manolin appears, at a tender age, to share that knowledge. That is part of his bond with Santiago. That is perhaps why he weeps at the old man's misfortune. He sees in what has happened more than just one more example of bad luck. He sees more than torn hands and a body racked by torturing exhaustion. He sees a parable of the human predicament unfolded before him and knows, with Santiago, that a man can only do what he must. He weeps, then, for joy at the glory of human tenacity, and he weeps for sorrow at the suffering a man must endure in the universe which is his home.

That is not simply the knowledge of the apprentice. It is the faith of the disciple whose master has initiated him into the mystery. Manolin's role is an integral part of the religious imagery of *The Old Man and the Sea*.

In the second place, the figure of Manolin makes an important contribution to the structure of the novel. Though he actually appears only in the prologue and the epilogue to the main story, he is never really absent from the narrative. During the time of Santiago's solitude upon the ocean, Manolin is referred to seven times. The references, of course, are not accidental. Examination of them helps in assessing the boy's contribution in structural terms.

1. The boy had given him two fresh small tunas, or albacores, which hung on the two deepest lines like plummets and, on the others, he had a big blue runner and a yellow jack that had been used before; but they were in good condition and had the excellent sardines to give them scent and attractiveness.

This passage, occurring at the beginning of the old man's voyage, is acknowledgement of the boy's contribution to the expedition. He has provided the important bait. Santiago does have some bait of his own—the blue runner and the yellow jack—but that bait is refreshed, as it were, by the boy's sardines. Moreover, the important bait, hung on the deepest lines, is the tuna, again given by Manolin. It is important bait because it is fresh.

There may be metaphorical implications in this passage, in that the boy's contribution to the voyage may be symbolic of his contribution to the life of the old man. Just as Manolin's bait brings the important quality of freshness to what the old man possesses, so he freshens the life of the old man. His youth feeds and revitalizes the old man's age. That is something which has happened already in the novel, as we can see from the conversation between the two. As they discuss the next day's voyage, Manolin offers practical help: he will obtain sardines for bait. However, equally interesting is the effect which his youthful enthusiasm has upon Santiago:

The old man looked at him with his sun-burned, confident loving eyes.
"If you were my boy I'd take you out and gamble," he said. "But you are your father's and your mother's and you are in a lucky boat."
"May I get the sardines? I know where I can get four baits too."
"I have mine left from today. I put them in salt in the box."
"Let me get four fresh ones."
"One," the old man said. His hope and his confidence had never gone. But now they were freshening as when the breeze rises.

Under the influence of the boy, Santiago's hope and confidence were "freshening." That is part of Manolin's function in the novel—the "freshening" of Santiago's age. Standing as it does at the threshold of the great adventure, the passage quoted above is probably indicative of that role.

2. The fish moved steadily and they travelled slowly on the calm water. The other baits were still in the water but there was nothing to be done.

"I wish I had the boy," the old man said aloud. "I'm being towed by a fish and I'm the towing bitt . . ."

This reference to Manolin, as other passages will make clear, becomes characteristic of Santiago's struggle with the great fish. His statement, "I wish I had the boy," is, on one level, a practical and straightforward expression of his desire for help. Were the boy with him, the other bait lines could be severed and thus nothing would interfere with the contest at hand. But another element, beyond that of mere practical function, appears in this scene. After his mention of the boy, the passage seems to move in a more positive direction. Santiago's thoughts become more positive as he abandons the negative aspects of what is happening to him. He thinks of what he must do: "I must hold him all I can and give him line when he must have it." He recognizes fortunate circumstances: "Thank God he is travelling and not going down." He abandons thought of unfortunate things that might happen and concentrates on what he is able to do: "But I'll do something. There are plenty of things I can do." As though mirroring his new frame of mind, he settles the line solidly against his back and watches the fish.

Thoughts of the boy have obviously accomplished something. The old man has received "freshening." His resolution has been renewed. Thus, mention of the boy has been more than an act of wishful thinking. It has been a kind of invocation which has found a response.

3. . . . Then he thought, think of it always. Think of what you are doing. You must do nothing stupid.

Then he said aloud, "I wish I had the boy. To help me and to see this."

No one should be alone in their old age, he thought. But it is unavoidable. I must remember to eat the tuna before he spoils in order to keep strong. Remember, no matter how little you want to, that you must eat him in the morning. Remember, he said to himself.

This reference to Manolin occurs at a time when the old man's thoughts are beginning to wander. He had concluded, moments earlier, that the fish and he had reached an impasse in their struggle: "I can do nothing with him and he can do nothing with me, he thought." Then he begins to think of baseball and wishes he had a radio in order to hear the latest scores. He becomes aware of his lack of concentration immediately. Thus, as though to revitalize himself once more, he invokes thoughts of Manolin. The effect is apparent at once. He becomes conscious of the problems of his age, and turns his mind to the practical consideration of eating in order to maintain his strength. Again, it would seem that an invocation has been uttered successfully, rather than mere wishful thinking being expressed with melancholy.

> **4.** "I wish the boy was here," he said aloud and settled himself against the rounded planks of the bow and felt the strength of the great fish through the line he held across his shoulders moving steadily toward whatever he had chosen.

Again the placement of this remark is interesting. Santiago has just recalled an incident from the past in which Manolin and he had hooked the female of a pair of marlin. Both he and the boy had been moved by the faithfulness of the marlin's mate, which had lingered with the boat and finally "jumped high into the air beside the boat to see where the female fish was." The moment had brought sadness to both the man and the boy. Thus, Santiago's expression of his desire to have the boy with him is again more than a plea for help. It is an expression of the communion of feeling they share. Significantly, once the communion has been expressed, the old man settles once more to the task at hand, and the qualities of the great marlin seem to flow into the fisherman. He feels the strength of the fish through the line across his shoulders and he feels the steadiness of the creature in its movements. Santiago's strength would appear to be revived, and he is able to settle to his work with renewed steadiness.

Once more, it would seem, thoughts of Manolin have worked their magic. The invocation has succeeded again.

> **5.** . . . How did I let the fish cut me with that one quick pull he made? I must be getting very stupid. Or perhaps I was looking at the small bird and thinking of him. Now I will pay attention to my work and then I must eat the tuna so that I will not have a failure of strength.
>
> "I wish the boy were here and that I had some salt," he said aloud.

This moment occurs after Santiago's dialogue with the small bird. Reflecting on the bird's fragility in a hostile universe, in which danger and death are ever-present threats, he has again failed to concentrate on his contest with the marlin. Consequently, when the fish gives a sudden lurch, the fisherman is unprepared and cuts his hand on the line. The experience turns his mind to practical concerns. He must, he realizes, maintain his strength. He must eat. But in the same instant he thinks of Manolin. The association of the boy with strength is inescapable. Manolin and strength are one. The association is confirmed by the words which follow: "I wish the boy were here and that I had some salt." The salt is needed to preserve and make more palatable the fish that the old man must eat to preserve his strength. It is, then, no accident that the boy and the salt are mentioned in the same breath. The salt takes on metaphorical connotations, indicative of the role which the boy plays. He is the source of strength, the seasoning for the old man's age, the means whereby Santiago is able to revive his flagging spirits and muster the resources of his weakening body.

Again, the reference to the boy is no vain utterance. It is the means by which Santiago is able to communicate with his source of strength and resolution.

6. If the boy were here he could rub it for me and loosen it down from the forearm, he thought. But it will loosen up.

This passage is probably best considered in conjunction with one which comes slightly later:

. . . But I will show him what a man can do and what a man endures.

"I told the boy I was a strange old man," he said. "Now is when I must prove it."

The thousand times that he had proved it meant nothing. Now he was proving it again. Each time was a new time and he never thought about the past when he was doing it.

The passages are alike in that neither is a direct invocation to the boy, as the foregoing passages were. Their effect, however, is similar to the incidents previously examined. In the first passage, Santiago is concerned about his cramped left hand. Were the boy in the boat, he could offer practical assistance; he could massage it and revive the circulation. The boy, of course, is not there, but the thought of him is effective enough. The old man is not dismayed. He is confident that his hand will loosen up and, later, warmed by the sun, his hand does lose its rigidity. Later still, when he needs to give consideration to his failing strength, it is thought of Manolin which brings him renewed resolve. He will prove himself for the boy. Each time, he declares, is a new time, and he is resolved to prove all that he has said to the boy.

Once more, the newness of strength that Manolin can bring to the old man's mind and body is vividly displayed. The refrain has been uttered again, if only in thought, and the energy of communion has flowed vigorously once more.

40

7. "I killed him in self-defense," the old man said aloud. "And I killed him well."

Besides, he thought, everything kills everything else in some way. Fishing kills me exactly as it keeps me alive. The boy keeps me alive, he thought. I must not deceive myself too much.

This passage is different in nature from the others. There is no incantation, no invocation of the spirit of the boy. It is a passage of direct and explicit acknowledgement. The boy, Santiago recognizes and admits, keeps him alive. There is no similar tribute elsewhere in the novel. This is the only occasion on which all that is unspoken between the man and the boy is uttered aloud. Their relationship, as we have seen, was built upon faith, and needed no words to express its quality. Now, alone upon the ocean, with his catch already torn by a shark, clearly aware of the hopelessness of encounters yet to come, Santiago utters the truth: "The boy keeps me alive."

The words surely express more than gratitude for Manolin's gifts of food and clothing and bait. They are an acknowledgement of all the strength that Manolin has contributed. His youth has fed the old man's age. His vigor—the splendid confidence and resolution of youth—has infused Santiago's body and spirit, warming the fires of his courage and his strength.

The invocations had done their work, and this final passage is Santiago's acknowledgement of that work.

Thus, it is clear that the relationship between Santiago and Manolin is an important aspect of the structure of *The Old Man and the Sea*. Manolin's role seems almost to create a small play in itself, which might be expressed schematically as follows:

ACT ONE: The Role Defined
ACT TWO: The Role in Action
ACT THREE: The Role Acknowledged

The figure of Manolin, then, is an important element in *The Old Man and the Sea*. It is true that the portrait is not particularized to any great extent. We learn little of Manolin as Manolin. There is an absence of those details which might make him a particular Cuban boy. His function would seem to be the significant thing about him. That function may be analyzed, according to the foregoing discussion, in the following way:

1. Manolin acts as a youthful reflection of the qualities of Santiago. He seems to share the same faith, the same humility, the same selflessness that are so strikingly portrayed in Santiago himself. Thus, the 'mirror image' helps Hemingway to emphasize the quality of life which the author is trying to portray in the old fisherman.

41

2. Manolin acts as a metaphor for all that is best in youth. The vigor and confidence and hopefulness shown by the boy are qualities which the old man knows to be important and which he seeks to revive in himself.

3. Manolin acts as an important ingredient in the religious context of the novel. As the earlier discussion of the character of Santiago has tried to make clear, that religious ingredient embodies more than orthodox concepts of religion. The old man is religious in the sense that he acts in accordance with a code of conduct which is clear and satisfying to him.

4. Manolin acts as an important element in the structural unity and tempo of the narrative. As the discussion has made clear, the boy is present—in spirit—at crucial moments in the narrative, and his 'presence' influences the action which ensues.

The Tourists

The tourists appear only briefly in the novel, and that appearance comes almost at the close of the book:

> That afternoon there was a party of tourists at the Terrace and looking down in the water among the empty beer cans and dead barracudas a woman saw a great long white spine with a huge tail at the end that lifted and swung with the tide while the east wind blew a heavy steady sea outside the entrance to the harbor.
>
> "What's that?" she asked a waiter and pointed to the long backbone of the great fish that was now just garbage waiting to go out with the tide.
>
> "Tiburon," the waiter said. "Eshark." He was meaning to explain what had happened.
>
> "I didn't know sharks had such handsome, beautifully formed tails."
>
> "I didn't either," her male companion said.

Brief though it is, this scene involving the tourists holds significant interest. They are obviously of little interest in themselves. The man and the woman who speak are hardly differentiated from the group to which they belong. It is their attitude which holds significance. They are only casually interested in the spine of the great fish, and their curiosity is simply a fleeting impulse. They ask the waiter for an explanation, yet they give him little chance to explain his brief reply. Thus, they are left with faulty information and no understanding of the magnitude of what has happened.

The tourists are evidently symbolic figures. They symbolize the attitude of all men who are spectators of the human scene rather than participants in its activity. They see, but they see without understanding. Only faintly curious, only passingly interested, only superficially observing, they have not been initiated into the mysteries that Santiago, Manolin and some of the older fisherman have apprehended. Tourists on vacation, they no doubt live life in tourist fashion, pecking at the surface of things without resolution, and never penetrating to the depths where mysteries are revealed.

Perhaps their attitude reflects the attitude of all people who live their lives ashore, who do not dare to grapple with the mysteries of life and death on the solitude of the ocean. The sea in literature is an ancient symbol for life, and men who launch out into the deep have frequently been portrayed as willing to grapple with the hidden meaning of human life. Hemingway seems to hint at this distinction between seafaring folk and the people of the shore in another passage in the novel, when Santiago, reflecting on the weather, says, "If there is a hurricane you always see the signs of it in the sky for days ahead, if you are at sea. They do not see it ashore because they do not know what to look for." The people ashore *do not know what to look for.* They are the blind; the seers are out upon the ocean.

Interestingly, Herman Melville, in *Moby Dick*, makes the same distinction between people of the shore and people of the sea. The sea, he suggests, does attract all men because of the lure of meaning, but only few dare to venture forth upon its waters:

> Circumambulate the city of a dreamy Sabbath afternoon. Go from Corlears Hook to Coenties Slip, and from thence, by Whitehall, northward. What do you see?—Posted like silent sentinels all around the town, stand thousands upon thousands of mortal men fixed in ocean reveries. Some leaning against the spiles; some seated upon the pier-heads; some looking over the bulwarks of ships from China; some high aloft in the rigging, as if striving to get a still better seaward peep. But these are all landsmen; of week days pent up in lath and plaster—tied to counters, nailed to benches, clinched to desks. How then is this? Are the green fields gone? What do they here? (Chapter I)

The picture is at once haunting and moving, for the people of the town represent all landsmen who vaguely discern possibilities of meaning, without being able to do anything to clutch it. Tied to the land, "pent up in lath and plaster," they can only yearn.

However, the plight of Hemingway's tourists is probably even worse. They do not yearn. They are blind, but are unconscious of their blindness. The mysteries are closed to them.

There are other characters in *The Old Man and the Sea*. However, they make no contribution in terms of meaning. Little more than names, and in some cases names only, they are on the periphery of

Santiago's life. For that reason, it is unnecessary to include them in this discussion of characters.

Structure

Commenting on the structure of *The Old Man and the Sea*, Dr. T. Goethals (*The Old Man and the Sea: A Critical Commentary.* New York: American R. D. M. Corp., 1965, p. 22) declares that the novel "contains a story—a story, note, not a plot. For, as E.M. Forster defined the difference many years ago, a plot requires an emphasis on causality, but a story is simply a 'narrative of events arranged in their time sequence.'" This judgment surely reflects a misreading of both E.M. Forster and *The Old Man and the Sea*.

Forster's distinction between narrative and plot is, of course, both useful and worthy. The distinction helps us to distinguish between the factual report and the artist's rendering of an event. There are stories in which the facts of events, the step-by-step unfolding of what happens, is the major interest. Most detective stories would fall into this category. They are intellectual puzzles, marvels of deductive logic, and the major interest focusses upon putting clues together successfully in order to discover the person responsible for a particular crime. Detective stories which have plot as well as narrative fall into a different category. For example, many of the books of Georges Simenon, with their emphasis upon human character and psychology, are more than detective stories; with plot, they become novels. They are not, then, merely a "narrative of events arranged in their time sequence." Thus, whenever bare narrative becomes only one element and the writer begins to occupy himself and his readers in deeper concerns—the irony of human existence, the complexity of human emotions, the resources of strength and weakness in human nature—what Forster calls "plot" is born.

Hence, to dismiss *The Old Man and the Sea* as story rather than plot is to do serious injustice to Hemingway's work. *The Old Man and the Sea* has a very carefully fashioned plot structure which helps to illuminate what Hemingway is endeavoring to say.

Dramatic Structure

The most obvious structural element in the novel is the dramatic structure. The narrative is carefully designed as a kind of drama in three acts.

The opening act is really a prologue, which sets forth the character of the central figure. Thus, there are only two characters in this section, Manolin and Santiago. The boy is used as a mirror to reflect the important qualities in the old man. Through their relationship, we gain insight into the qualities of character and the habits of mind of Santiago.

The second 'act' forms the bulk of Hemingway's drama. In this section, the main elements of the narrative are the hooking of the marlin, the chase, the capture, and the attacks by the sharks. Careful reading will reveal that this part of the drama has a skilfully woven texture. The narrative has rhythms which are created by a subtle weaving of action, meditation and recollection. Its dramatic unity is derived from a number of minor structural elements: Santiago's overriding determination to bring the fish home to port; the careful fixing of the time at each stage; the description of the old man's precise manoeuvres at critical moments in the battle; the shrewdly calculated appearances of various ocean 'characters'; and the ebb and flow of the old man's strength and resolution. The total effect is dramatic.

The last section of the novel is markedly cinematic in technique. It is composed of several short scenes and the eye of the camera, as it were, shifts its focus swiftly as one short 'scene' follows another. Thus, there is, first of all, the old man's arrival at the harbor, and the camera follows him steadily as he makes his way agonizingly to his shack. The 'scene' ends with an unmoving focus upon Santiago slumped on the bed, his arms out-stretched and the palms of his hands facing up. In the following incident, the time has changed to the next morning, as Manolin visits his friend. Quickly, the setting moves to the harbor. Equally swiftly, the narrative returns to the shack, and there is talk of the future. Following this, the time changes to afternoon, and the focus is fixed upon a group of tourists. When that brief movement is over, we are transported to the shack once more, where the final 'scene' is a tableau with the old man asleep and the boy sitting silently by him. Clearly, this last 'act' of the drama is a vivid illustration of the power of economy in Hemingway's work. Seven short scenes follow one another rapidly, each making its contribution to our insight and understanding. The details are sparse, but the impact is great. The dramatic quality of the narrative is clearly evident.

Plainly, *The Old Man and the Sea* is, in structural terms, a drama. The events which make up the story are composed in a manner which is based solidly upon chronology, but which also reveal a shrewd shifting of focus and a subtle alternation of rhythms. The result is much more than a story. Rather, it is drama that is complex and sophisticated.

Structure through Tempo

In discussing the role played in the narrative by Manolin and the references to young lions, Carlos Baker discerns a basic rhythm in *The Old Man and the Sea*, a rhythm which he describes as "the constant wavelike operation of bracing and relaxation." Thus, in his view, thoughts of the boy brace Santiago, firming his resolution, while the lions relax him, calming his anxieties. Consequently, Baker affirms, a characteristic rhythm can be identified in the novel:

. . . In its maritime sections, at any rate, the basic rhythms of the novel resemble those of the ground swell of the sea. Again and again as the action unfolds, the reader may find that he is gradually brought up to a degree of quiet tension just barely endurable, as in the ascent by a small craft of a slow enormous wave. When he has reached the presumptive peak of his resistance, the crest passes and he suddenly relaxes towards a trough of rest. The rhythm of the story appears to be built on such a stress-yield, brace-relax alternation. ("Hemingway's Ancient Mariner," in *Ernest Hemingway: Critiques of Four Major Novels*, p. 157)

A detailed examination of the narrative in the central section of the novel seems to support a conclusion of the kind Baker makes. There is not always a boy/lions alternation, but there is a rhythmic alternation of meditation and action that is constant and regular. There are five critical moments associated with the marlin, and the pattern of the narrative following each of these five moments reveals the rhythmic structure of the narrative.

The first crucial moment is the taking of the bait: "He's taken it," he said. "Now I'll let him eat it well." The pattern of the events which follow is easily analyzed:

ACTION: to lodge the hook securely, Santiago pulls hard on the line, though with little success. He settles the line across his shoulders and prepares for a long struggle.

THE BOY: for the first time, Santiago expresses his need for Manolin.

RESOLUTION: thoughts of the boy are succeeded by a quickening of Santiago's resolve to endure: "But I'll do something. There are plenty of things I can do."; "You must do nothing stupid."

THE BOY: needing to strengthen his determination, Santiago once more calls upon the boy.

MEDITATION: thoughts of Manolin appear to soothe the old man, and he reflects on a previous experience they had shared, the killing of one of a pair of marlin.

THE BOY: thoughts of that earlier experience bring sadness to the old man, and again he declares, "I wish the boy was here."

ACTION: moved to action, Santiago severs the bait lines.

THE BOY: conscious of the problems facing him, Santiago once more thinks of Manolin: "I wish I had the boy."

ACTION: resolved anew, the old man finishes his work with the bait lines, and settles to the struggle: "I can do it as long as he can." ". . . I will kill you dead before this day ends."

MEDITATION: the visit to the skiff of a small bird moves Santiago to a tender, reflective soliloquy which is interrupted suddenly by the unexpected lurching of the great fish.

Even a brief examination of these pages reveals a pattern in the narrative which seems to be made up of a crisis/ boy/ action/ meditation alternation. The same movement may be detected by study of other critical moments involving the struggle with the marlin: the lurching of the fish; the emergence of the fish; the jumping of the great fish; and the marlin's attack on the line.

One may regard it as over-fanciful and too poetic to claim, with Baker, that "the basic rhythms of the novel resemble those of the ground swell of the sea." Nonetheless, a pattern is discernible in the narrative, and the events do appear to ebb and flow according to the alternation described earlier. It is a perceptible movement, however we may choose to describe it, and it does give the novel a characteristic tempo which contributes to the structural unity.

Structure by Means of Motif

The word 'motif' is most commonly used in music to describe the way in which a recurring musical phrase may be used by the composer to signal key moments in his composition—a change of mood, a shift in idea, a movement in tempo, and so on. The same term is used in similar fashion in literature. Frequently, a writer uses recurring references to a person or a thing or an idea to signal crucial or characteristic moments in his narrative. These people or things or ideas then assume a function which goes far beyond their ordinary meaning. The repetitions, and the contexts in which the repetitions occur, add connotations which may contribute significantly to the author's themes. The people or things or ideas are then usually described as images, and the patterning of the appearances of the image becomes the 'motif'.

As these Notes explain elsewhere (see IMAGERY), there are two major *motifs* in the central section of *The Old Man and the Sea*: the boy and the lions.

The boy, Manolin, is a major motif, whether or not we subscribe to Baker's theory of "bracing." He is mentioned explicitly seven times in the central portion of the novel. An eighth significant reference to Manolin occurs after Santiago's first battle with a shark. These references to the boy almost constitute a play within a play, for they have their own beginning, middle and ending.

The first reference appears to be an explicit statement of the boy's role in symbolic terms. Manolin, we are told, had given the old man "two small fresh tunas," and his further gift of sardines gave Santiago's bait "scent and attractiveness." Santiago's old bait, it is clear, is freshened by Manolin's gift. The freshness is not insignificant. The term could well be seen as relating to the effect of Manolin on the old man in the early stages of the novel where, in conversation with the boy, Santiago's hope and confidence "were freshening as when the breeze rises." Thus, the boy comes to represent the renewal of the old man's youthful energies. Manolin is the leavening ingredient which will cause Santiago's waning power and resolve to rise in response to the demands made upon him.

The six succeeding references bear out the justness of this thesis. Strengthened by his thoughts of the boy, the old man is able to abandon his troubled thoughts about the bait lines and apply himself with quickened resolve to the things that he can and must do: "There are plenty of things I can do." Later, his resolve weakening—"I can do nothing with him and he can do nothing with me."—and his concentration wandering, thoughts of Manolin enable him to turn to the practical consideration of eating in order to maintain his strength. Later still, overcome by sadness, two references to the boy, occurring so closely together that they can be interpreted as the same reference, give Santiago the determination he needs to sever the last bait line and hook up the two reserve coils of line. On the fifth occasion that he mentions the boy, Santiago has again slackened his concentration by talking to the small bird which visited his craft. A sudden lurch by the marlin injures the fisherman, and he again wishes that the boy were with him. Santiago's words convey clearly the association of the boy with new reserves of strength: "I wish the boy were here and that I had some salt." The two following references to Manolin reveal the same pattern of cause and effect. In both cases, Santiago is acutely aware of his failing strength. In both cases, the result is renewed resolve, as Santiago makes clear:

> "I told the boy I was a strange old man," he said. "Now is when I must prove it."
> The thousand times that he had proved it meant nothing. Now he was proving it again. Each time was a new time and he never thought about the past when he was doing it.

The final reference is Santiago's acknowledgement of Manolin's great gift, which is more than food and other necessities. The boy brings the gift of life itself: "The boy keeps me alive, he thought. I must not deceive myself too much."

And so the minor drama is played out within the major drama. The motif created by Manolin is evidently a major thread in the central portion of the narrative, weaving its subtle way through the rhythms of Santiago's struggle with the marlin and contributing dramatically to the ebb and flow of the action. Manolin is thus more than a little Cuban boy whose presence lends an air of pathos to the figure of Santiago. He plays a major role in the structure of the novel as the qualities of his youth infuse the waning physical and spiritual energies of the old man with quickened vitality and renewed resolve. He is, then, more than a character; he becomes an important motif.

The lions comprise a second major motif. They are mentioned

early in the story, as the old man sleeps on the night before his momentous voyage:

> He was asleep in a short time and he dreamed of Africa when he was a boy and the long golden beaches and the white beaches, so white they hurt your eyes, and the high capes and the great brown mountains. He lived along that coast now every night and in his dreams he heard the surf roar and saw the native boats come riding through it. He smelled the tar and oakum of the deck as he slept and he smelled the smell of Africa that the land breeze brought at morning. . . .
>
> He no longer dreamed of storms, nor of women, nor of great occurrences, nor of great fish, nor fights, nor contests of strength, nor of his wife. He only dreamed of places now and of the lions on the beach. They played like young cats in the dusk and he loved them as he loved the boy. He never dreamed about the boy.

The inferences in this passage are clear and important. To begin with, we note that the lions are the substance of Santiago's dreams and, thereby, are associated with the restfulness of sleep. They thus take on the restful, relaxing, energy-reviving qualities of sleep. It is important also to observe the connection between the lions and youth. They are part of the Africa Santiago knew as a boy. The lions, therefore, become associated with the energetic, hopeful, confident qualities of youth. This association is confirmed by an earlier remark of Santiago when, talking to Manolin, he observes, "When I was your age I was before the mast on a square rigged ship that ran to Africa and I have seen lions on the beaches in the evening." In this remark, the association of the lions with youth is deepened by the parallel between Santiago's age then and Manolin's age now. All of this obviously indicates the significance of the lions as an image of youth which brings content and restfulness to the old man. The concept is not complex or startling, and it has been observed by a number of critics, notably by Carlos Baker.

There is one further noteworthy element in the passage quoted. Hemingway states explicitly that "He never dreamed about the boy." The statement is interesting, though not difficult to understand or interpret. It makes a clear distinction between Manolin as an image of youth and the lions as an image of youth. The lions belong to the past; they were the creatures of the old man's younger days. He gains strength from them through the act of reflection. The boy, however, belongs to the present, and the present demands action. Santiago must prove himself again *now* for the sake of the boy and all that they share. The past does not demand urgent action; the present does. It is from this difference that Baker develops his theory of bracing and relaxation in describing the rhythm of the central section of *The Old Man and the Sea*. Certainly, examination of the context in which the references to the lions occur suggests that, as an image, they create a different mood and tone from those aroused by the boy.

When Santiago first mentions the lions on his voyage, he has just summoned all of his resolution to prove himself again for Manolin's sake. He would show himself to be "a strange old man." At once, he thinks of the lions:

> I wish he'd sleep and I could sleep and dream about the lions, he thought. Why are the lions the main thing that is left? Don't think, old man, he said to himself. Rest gently now against the wood and think of nothing. He is working. Work as little as you can.

The old man's shift from hardy resolve to thoughts of pleasurable restfulness is psychologically credible. At his age, the old flames of courage can be relit, but the temptation of ease is real. Perhaps in his weariness and solitude it is fitting that Santiago should desire peace. Perhaps, to one in his condition, the lions do seem to be all that is left. They are the image of a glorious time that was and is no more, and the old man yearns, in the present crisis, to be left with his dreams.

Later, the old man's wish is granted. He dreams of his beloved lions:

> After that he began to dream of the long yellow beach and he saw the first of the lions come down onto it in the early dark and then the other lions came and he rested his chin on the wood of the bows where the ship lay anchored with the evening off-shore breeze and he waited to see if there would be more lions and he was happy.

Thought of the lions occurs as the fisherman is preparing to rest. He is feeling a little more relaxed and confident. He has eaten; the weather signs are favorable; and he has settled himself as comfortably as possible against the bow. Sleep follows naturally and, equally naturally, the dream of the lions comes. The image reflects his mood: ". . . he was happy." Thoughts of Manolin do not seem to have the same effect. His words concerning the boy are usually followed immediately by action. Here, the lions indicate a more relaxed state of being, which is interrupted only by the sudden jerking of the fish.

The final reference to the lions occurs in the last paragraph of the novel:

> Up the road, in his shack, the old man was sleeping again. He

was still sleeping on his face and the boy was sitting by watching him. The old man was dreaming about the lions.

Here, past and present meet in the conjunction of the boy and the lions. The old man has made his plans for the future, and Manolin has shared in them: "I will have everything in order." The boy's function is clear: he is the unavoidable present in which the depths of human heroism must be proved and proved again, and he is the promise of the future, which can be looked forward to with confidence and expectation. But for the old man, the past is never far away. His strength comes also from the recollection of what has been. Refreshed by sleep, he will no doubt be refreshed by his memories of the past.

The motif of the lions appears much less frequently than the motif involving Manolin. That fact need cause no surprise. It is, after all, psychologically convincing. On the ocean, Santiago is faced by a series of crises whose import is not lost upon him. He is called upon to demonstrate what a man can endure. It is demanded of him that he show that a man cannot be defeated. He is resolved to prove himself once more. In such an hour, Santiago needs a power to revive him and a spirit to renew him. That power and that spirit are provided by Manolin, the young boy. It is thus appropriate that references to Manolin occur so frequently. The references to the lions are, in contrast, few because in some way they are a seductive image. They represent the temptation of reflective ease, a temptation attractive to a weary old man. In the second place, however, the difference in frequency between the two sets of images is, from Hemingway's point of view, also artistically convincing. The Hemingway *credo* emphasizes the strength of the inner man as demonstrated in action. All that is best in the qualities of youth can, in this view, be revived and exercised again. The boy, a present image of youthful reality, is a much more fitting expression of this belief than are the lions, reflective as they are of the past.

Clearly, the structure of *The Old Man and the Sea* is a sophisticated creation. There is more involved than mere chronology. The subtle interplay of reflection, rest and action is complex and absorbing. Three elements in that interplay—drama, tempo and motif—have been examined in detail here. However, a word of caution is necessary.

The elements are there, but they are skilfully woven together. They are not separate and distinct. They blend together to form the distinctive creation that is the narrative of *The Old Man and the Sea* and evoke the response from the reader which recognizes the work as haunting and moving.

Style

Introduction

Hemingway's style is distinctive. Its features are clearly recognizable and its techniques readily identifiable. However, the distinctiveness has not been universally praised. Many critics have criticized Hemingway, often on the basis of style alone. Thus, Harry Levin ("Observations on the Style of Ernest Hemingway," in *Hemingway and His Critics,* edited by Carlos Baker) pungently presents what may be regarded as the faults of Hemingway's style. Hemingway's diction, he declares, is thin, his syntax is weak, and "he would rather be caught dead than seeking the *mot juste* or the balanced phrase." Leslie Fiedler is even more critical:

> . . . The single flaw in *The Old Man and the Sea* is the constant sense that Hemingway is no longer creating, but merely imitating the marvelous spare style that was once a revelation; that what was once an anti-rhetoric has become now merely another rhetoric, perhaps our most familiar one, and that even its inventor cannot revive it for us. (Quoted in *Twentieth Century Interpretations of The Old Man and the Sea*, edited by Katharine T. Jobes, p. 108)

Nemi D'Agostino is no less hard-hitting:

> . . . A late work by a tired writer who believes more than ever in the religion of beauty, its subtly mannered idiom, its elegant and frozen rhythms, are separated by the space of a whole lifetime from the lucid movement, the fresh and crystalline clarity, the poignancy and the shock-power of the language of the young Hemingway. (*Ibid*, p. 109)

Yet the very faults that some have singled out for blame have been praised as virtues by others. In his book on Hemingway, Stewart Sanderson praises what he calls "the simple prose and richly poetic conception of *The Old Man and the Sea*." (p. 118) Mark Schorer echoes the praise:

> . . . For this appears to be not only a moral fable, but a parable, and all the controlled passion in the story, all the taut excitement in the prose, come, I believe, from the parable. It is an old man catching a fish, yes, but it is also a great artist in the act of mastering his subject, and, more than that, of actually writing about that struggle. Nothing is more important than his craft, and it is beloved; but because it must be struggled with and mastered, it is also a foe, enemy

to all self-indulgence, to all looseness of feeling, all laxness of style, all soft pomposities. ("With Grace Under Pressure," in *Ernest Hemingway: Critiques of Four Major Novels,* edited by Carlos Baker, p. 134)

These conflicting interpretations of Hemingway's style obviously present a problem. It is a problem not readily solved. In the end, one can only consider the evidence carefully and come to a conclusion, based on common sense, taste and reason, which one finds personally valid and satisfying.

Hemingway's View on Style

A. From "An Interview with Ernest Hemingway"

"If a writer stops observing he is finished. But he does not have to observe consciously nor think how it will be useful. Perhaps that would be true at the beginning. But later everything he sees goes into the great reserve of things he knows or has seen. If it is any use to know it, I always try to write on the principle of the iceberg. There is seven-eighths of it under water for every part that shows. Anything you know you can eliminate and it only strengthens your iceberg. It is the part that doesn't show. If a writer omits something because he does not know it then there is a hole in the story.

"*The Old Man and the Sea* could have been over a thousand pages long and had every character in the village in it and all the processes of how they made their living, were born, educated, bore children, etc. That is done excellently and well by other writers. In writing you are limited by what has already been done satisfactorily. So I have tried to learn to do something else. I have tried to eliminate everything unnecessary to conveying experience to the reader so that after he or she has read something it will become a part of his or her experience and seem actually to have happened. This is very hard to do and I've worked at it very hard.

"Anyway, to skip how it is done, I had unbelievable luck this time and could convey the experience completely and have it be one that no one had ever conveyed. The luck was that I had a good man and a good boy and lately writers have forgotten there still are such things. Then the ocean is worth writing about just as man is. So I was lucky there. I've seen the marlin mate and know about that. So I leave that out. I've seen a school (or pod) of more than fifty sperm whales in that same stretch of water and once harpooned one nearly sixty feet in length and lost him. So I left that out. All the stories I know from the fishing village I leave out. But the knowledge is what makes the underwater part of the iceberg."

B. From *Death in the Afternoon*

"Prose is architecture, not interior decoration, and the Baroque is over. For a writer to put his own intellectual musings, which he might sell for a low price as essays, into the mouths of artificially constructed characters which are more remunerative when issued as people in a novel is good economics, perhaps, but does not make literature. People in a novel, not skillfully constructed *characters*, must be projected from the writer's assimilated experience, from his knowledge, from his head, from his heart and from all there is of him. If he ever has luck as well as seriousness and gets them out entire they will have more than one dimension and they will last a long time. A good writer should know as near everything as possible. Naturally he will not. A great enough writer seems to be born with knowledge. But he really is not; he has only been born with the ability to learn in a quicker ratio to the passage of time than other men and without conscious application, and with an intelligence to accept or reject what is already presented as knowledge. There are some things which cannot be learned quickly and time, which is all we have, must be paid heavily for their acquiring. They are the very simplest things and because it takes a man's life to know them, the little new that each man gets from life is very costly and the only heritage he has to leave. Every novel which is truly written contributes to the total of knowledge which is there at the disposal of the next writer who comes, but the next writer must pay, always, a certain nominal percentage in experience to be able to understand and assimilate what is available as his birthright and what he must, in turn, take his departure from. If a writer of prose knows enough about what he is writing about he may omit things that he knows and the reader, if the writer is writing truly enough, will have a feeling of those things as strongly as though the writer had stated them. The dignity of movement of an iceberg is due to only one-eighth of it being above water. A writer who omits things because he does not know them only makes hollow places in his writing. A writer who appreciates the seriousness of writing so little that he is anxious to make people see he is formally educated, cultured or well-bred is merely a popinjay. And this too remember: a serious writer is not to be confounded with a solemn writer. A serious writer may be a hawk or a buzzard or even a popinjay, but a solemn writer is always a bloody owl."

The Old Man and the Sea

In writing of style, Hemingway repeats the analogy of the iceberg, which drifts in the ocean with only one-eighth of its vastness showing. The writer, he affirms, must be in some way like that. He does not need to show all that he knows, but if he truly knows, the reader will enter into that knowledge, for it will be implicit in what has been written. At its best, this approach to writing results in prose which has the *clarity* of crystal while, at the same time, being richly evocative in its suggestions. The opening paragraph of *The Old Man and the Sea* surely achieves this clarity:

> He was an old man who had fished alone in a skiff in the Gulf Stream and he had gone eighty-four days now without taking a fish. In the first forty days a boy had been with him. But after forty days without a fish the boy's parents had told him that the old man was now definitely and finally *salao*, which is the worst form of unlucky, and the boy had gone at their orders in another boat which caught three good fish the first week. It made the boy sad to see the old man come in each day with his skiff empty and he always went down to help him carry either the coiled lines or the gaff and harpoon and the sail that was furled around the mast. The sail was patched with flour sacks and, furled, it looked like the flag of permanent defeat.

The conception is clear and unmuddied by adornment and embellishment. The only obvious literary device—the simile in the last sentence—is simple, a simplicity emphasized by the detail of flour sacks.

The clarity is achieved through both the simplicity of the diction and the *economy* of the words. The economy is characteristic of Hemingway, and enables him to convey particularly well a sense of action through the medium of the visual. Examples of this achievement are numerous in *The Old Man and the Sea*. Two such examples will suffice for present purposes. In the first scene, Santiago catches a tuna for food:

> . . . Just then the stern line came taut under his foot, where he had kept a loop of the line, and he dropped his oars and felt the weight of the small tuna's shivering pull as he held the line firm and commenced to haul it in. The shivering increased as he pulled in and he could see the blue back of the fish in the water and the gold of his sides before he swung him over the side and into the boat. He lay in the stern in the sun, compact and bullet shaped, his big, unintelligent eyes staring as he thumped his life out against the planking of the boat with the quick shivering strokes of his neat, fast-moving tail.

In the second scene, Santiago kills his great adversary:

> The old man dropped the line and put his foot on it and lifted the harpoon as high as he could and drove it down with all his strength, and more strength he had just summoned, into the fish's side just behind the great chest fin that rose high in the

air to the altitude of the man's chest. He felt the iron go in and he leaned on it and drove it further and then pushed all his weight after it.

Lean and sinewy, the prose in such episodes is far from flowery embellishment and serves well to give us a sense of emotion in action.

Faced in *The Old Man and the Sea* with the problem of making the common uncommon, the ordinary extraordinary, Hemingway seems to have approached his task with an extraordinary *control in diction*. The Cuban setting, just remote enough from common experience, is shrewdly sketched. The few phrases of Spanish in the novel communicate well the exotic nature of the experience, without troubling the reader with their strangeness, and the diction in dialogue is, on the whole, crafted carefully so that it is credible as the words of peasants.

The greatest achievement, however, is probably in the creation of the parable-like quality of the narrative. As has frequently been observed, the book reminds us of the language of the Bible. The effect, of course, is not accidental. It has been achieved by means of skilled craftsmanship in the *rhythms* and *sentence structure*. The sentences flow, not in the fashion of formal utterances shaped according to the patterns of traditional rhetoric, but in the fashion characteristic of the rhythms of speech:

> But after forty days without a fish the boy's parents had told him that the old man was now definitely and finally *salao*, which is the worst form of unlucky, and the boy had gone at their orders in another boat which caught three good fish the first week.
>
> • • •
>
> They were strange shoulders, still powerful although very old, and the neck was still strong too and the creases did not show so much when the old man was asleep and his head fallen forward.
>
> • • •
>
> The boy was sad too and we begged her pardon and butchered her promptly.

These utterances, and many others in the novel, achieve their haunting cadence, not by means of an artificially imposed pattern dictated by laws of rhetoric, but by means of the informal rhythms of speech, with its irregular alternation of stressed and unstressed syllables. The result is poetic prose with the rhythms we have learned to associate with the language of parables.

Finally, a distinctive feature in the writing of *The Old Man and the Sea* is Hemingway's frequent association of affirmation and negation. Declarations of confidence rub shoulders with evidence of doom. The negative accompanies the positive. That close association gives the narrative the *irony* which its message announces. Examples are numerous:

> This will kill him, the old man thought. He can't do this forever. But four hours later the fish was still swimming steadily out to sea, towing the skiff, and the old man was still braced solidly with the line across his back.
>
> • • •
>
> "Fish," he said softly, aloud, "I'll stay with you until I am dead."
> He'll stay with me too, I suppose, the old man thought and he waited for it to be light.
>
> • • •
>
> "But I will kill you dead before this day ends." Let us hope so, he thought.

The irony, of course, is part of the theme, which shows us the paradox of a man who is beaten and yet not defeated. The style, then, is in part what it should be—a metaphor for theme.

Imagery

In literature, when a character, object or idea becomes powerfully associated with a particular set of connotations or possible significances which extend beyond the limits imposed by simple representation, description or exposition, the character, object or idea is usually described as an image. The thing becomes more than the thing itself; it becomes a bearer of meanings. At a second stage, when a particular image is repeated with similar connotations, it takes on the characteristics of a motif. In the final stage, when the correspondence between the image and its connotations is most clearly defined, the image becomes a symbol.

Obviously, the use of imagery is an important technique for the writer. Through imagery, he can, first of all, enrich the texture of his writing. That is not to imply that imagery is mere adornment, that its function is largely to "dress up" the writing. Rather, in the hands of the skilful, sensitive writer, the imagery is embedded in the texture and creates echoes of meaning which make a vivid, meaningful contribution to what is written. Such is the case with *The Old Man and the Sea*, in which various groups of images combine to make the novel an evocative narrative.

For the convenience of the student, the images of the novel have been considered in series, so that they can more easily be understood and analyzed.

The Boy

It is unnecessary at this point to analyze exhaustively the function of Manolin as a recurrent image. That has been accomplished elsewhere (see CHARACTERS and STRUCTURE). It is sufficient, at this stage, to summarize the contributions which the boy makes in terms of imagery.

In the first place, Manolin helps to affirm one of the themes of the novel. In part, *The Old Man and the Sea* confronts the problem of age. Given the view of man which Hemingway seems to present, the protagonist is faced with the problem of demonstrating his essential manhood at a period of his life when his physical powers are waning and the resources of his resolve are questionable. Yet he must prove himself. That is his only true response to a universe that is, at best, neutral. It would be easier and more comfortable, in such circumstances, to rest on past achievements, gained at a time of youthful vigor and courage. It would be easier and more comfortable, in such circumstances, to devote one's self to contented recollection of past glories. The image of the lions may, in part, convey the seductive enchantment of such a response. But for the Hemingway hero, such a response is impossible. It is impossible because it is a betrayal of all that it means to be a man. Thus, Santiago, tempted by thoughts of tranquil recollection, is aroused continually by the image of Manolin. The boy is the representation of all the youthful powers that the old man can find within himself. Man is not the external, physical being alone; he is what he is by virtue of his inner qualities. Manolin revives those inner powers.

Second, the image of Manolin, recurring powerfully and insistently so that the image becomes a motif, contributes significantly to the structure of the novel. That contribution is two-fold. On the one hand, it is a contribution in terms of action. Manolin trigger Santiago's resolve and, thereby, he is able to do those things which are necessary to defeat the great marlin. On the other hand, Manolin plays an important part in the rhythmic structure of the novel. As has been discussed in detail elsewhere (see STRUCTURE), the boy has a significant role in the ebb and flow of the action in the central portion of *The Old Man and the Sea.*

The Lions

The image of the lions has also been discussed in detail elsewhere in these *Notes* (see STRUCTURE). Their significance as image does not need to be established again. It is useful to reiterate, however, the nature of their function as an image.

First, as with the image of the boy, they are a part of the youth/old age theme of the novel. Their appearance signals the seductive nostalgia of the old man as he drifts into sleep. Always appearing at night (in sleep), as in the dream they always appeared on the beach in the evening, they are symbolic in Santiago's thoughts, for he is at the evening of his life, and they express a wistful yearning for the vigor and splendor that are no more. Even this function, though, may not be wholly passive. There may not be in these moments only nostalgia. For the lions also indicate the undying hope and confidence within a man. The image does not die or wane, and thus may also represent the very real presence of resources upon which the old man can still draw.

Second, again, as with the boy, the lions form part of the rhythmic structure of *The Old Man and the Sea*. As the tide of the action shifts and moves, the references to the lions create a tempo which alternates with that created by the marlin's actions and by Santiago's recollections of Manolin.

Religious Imagery

The largest group of images in the novel is that of the religious images.

Most obvious is the parallel between Santiago and Christ. The old man exhibits many of the qualities which are usually regarded as Christ-like. He has powerful conviction—frequently expressed as faith and pride—and true humility. More striking still, however, is the parallel between the sufferings of Santiago and the sufferings of Christ. Thus, as Santiago wrestles with his fish, his suffering is physical as well as spiritual. His left hand is rendered useless by cramp and his right hand is torn by the line, and his back is bruised by the rope which is braced around his shoulders. These injuries are, of course, reminiscent of the experience of Jesus, who was scourged and then nailed through his hands to the cross. When a pair of menacing sharks is sighted, the correspondence becomes even closer, as the following passage makes clear:

> "*Ay*," he said aloud. There is no translation for this word and perhaps it is just a noise such as a man might make, involuntarily, feeling the nail go through his hands and into the wood.

Just so, it is said, on his cross Jesus also gave a cry which is interpreted in various ways. The parallel is equally evident at the end of the novel. Arriving in the harbor late at night, Santiago "shouldered the mast and started to climb." He then knew "the depth of his tiredness," just as in shouldering his cross Jesus must have known the bitter depths of his experience after a night of interrogation and punishment. As the old man climbed to his shack, he stumbled and fell—seven times in all—even as Jesus stumbled in carrying his cross. When Santiago reached home at last, he "found a water bottle and took a drink," just as Christ on the cross was given a drink. Totally exhausted, the old man "pulled the blanket over his shoulders and then over his back and legs and he slept face down on the newspapers with his arms out straight and the palms of his hands up.'' Santiago's final pose is that of the crucified man, and the parallel with Christ is confirmed in visual terms. In addition to all of this, when we realize that it is noon on the first day out that the old man hooks the marlin and noon on the third day that he kills his adversary, the firm chronology is also reminiscent of the crucifixion experience of Jesus.

The evidence needs to be interpreted carefully, however. If the correspondence between Santiago and Christ is interpreted as being total and exact, then *The Old Man and the Sea* becomes a religious allegory in which Santiago is the symbol of Christ. However, the identification is not complete. First, we must accept the old man's affirmation that he is not religious. His attitude to God, witnessed in his prayers and his references to God, would certainly not appear to be that of a man we would ordinarily describe as pious. Significantly, also, the religious pictures in Santiago's shack belonged, not to him, but to his wife. Further, the nature of the old man's resolution is hardly Christlike: ''I love you and respect you very much. But I will kill you dead before this day ends.'' Finally, in killing the fish, Santiago, as Joseph Waldmeir has pointed out, more nearly resembles a picture of a matador finishing off a bull than that of one who is crucified:

> The old man dropped the line and put his foot on it and lifted the harpoon as high as he could and drove it down with all his strength, and more strength he had just summoned, into the fish's side just behind the great chest fin that rose high in the air to the altitude of the man's chest. He felt the iron go in and he leaned on it and drove it further and then pushed all his weight after it.

The parallel between Santiago and Christ is obviously intended to be less than total identification. Any other conclusion would not be in accord with Hemingway's philosophy of human existence. The parallel in the religious imagery moves towards two other accomplishments. On one level, the religious imagery contributes to the artistic effect of the novel, which in its style is reminiscent of biblical parables. On a second level, the evocation of the experience of Christ enables Hemingway to emphasize the heroic mould in which Santiago is cast. Conviction, resolution, stoicism—all are characteristics of Jesus, and all are heroic in nature.

The numbers which occur in the novel are also part of the fabric of the religious imagery. From earliest times, numbers have been associated with hidden meanings, most of which are lost in antiquity. Nevertheless, signs of the mystical process are abundant in, for example, both the Old Testament and the New Testament. Three, four, seven and forty, together with their multiples, have sacred significance.

For example, three was a sacred number in early Babylonian religious cults, and appears in the New Testament in the concept of the Trinity. Four was thought of as a symbol of perfection through its pictorial representation as a square, and YHWH (Yahweh), the Hebrew name for God, contained four letters. The number, seven, is probably the most common of the Hebrew sacred numbers and appears, best known, in the concept of Creation being completed on the seventh day. The last number, forty, is mentioned as the time that Moses spent leading the Jews through the Sinai and also as the period of time during which Jesus fought temptation in the wilderness. There are, of course, more sacred numbers which had special significance for ancient peoples. The four which have been mentioned—3, 4, 7, 40—are stressed here because they are found in *The Old Man and the Sea*. Thus, Santiago's contest with the great marlin lasted for three days. Before his gruelling experience, the old man had fished for forty days in the company of Manolin, without success. He had also fished since then without success for forty-four more days. The number seven is involved in three critical incidents: the great marlin, from the moment of grasping the hook to the moment of his last, desperate jump, challenges the fisherman seven times; Santiago kills seven sharks; and from the harbor to the floor of his shack, the old man is forced to lay down the mast of the skiff seven times. As numbers, they have no significance in themselves or any significance of an absolute sort. But they do form a motif which, like the parallel between Santiago and Christ, emphasizes the parable-like quality of the narrative and associates it with biblical qualities.

The Ocean and the Marlin

The relationship between Santiago and the marlin is more than that between the hunter and the hunted, between the pursuer and the pursued. A careful reading of the 'chase' section of the book reveals shifts and developments in the relationship which are at once intriguing and significant.

As the old man begins his quest on the eighty-fifth day, his feelings are probably best expressed in the words of Manolin: "It is what a man must do." Thus, when Santiago first hooks the fish, his thoughts reflect only his attitude of acceptance. The situation is familiar and inevitable, and he feels no emotion other than hopeful expectation as he coaxes his prey to take the hook: "Make another turn. Just smell them. Aren't they lovely? Eat them good now and then there is the tuna. Hard and cold and lovely. Don't be shy, fish. Eat them." His thoughts and emotions are concentrated solely upon the act that must be performed:

Eat it so that the point of the hook goes into your heart and kills you, he thought. Come up easy and let me put the harpoon into you. All right. Are you ready? Have you been long enough at table?

"Now!" he said aloud and struck hard with both hands, gained a yard of line and then struck again and again, swinging with each arm alternately on the cord with all the strength of his arms and the pivoted weight of his body.

When he fails to master the fish immediately and it begins to tow his skiff, Santiago begins to think in terms different from those suggested by the relationship between hunter and hunted. He now longs to see the fish "to know what I have against me," and he recognizes the equality inherent in the encounter: "I can do nothing with him and he can do nothing with me . . ."

In the next stage of the battle, Santiago feels pity for the marlin and speculates about its nature:

. . . He is wonderful and strange and who knows how old he is, he thought. Never have I had such a strong fish nor one who acted so strangely. Perhaps he is too wise to jump. He could ruin me by jumping or by a wild rush. But perhaps he has been hooked many times before and he knows that this is how he should make his fight. He cannot know that it is only one man against him, nor that it is an old man. But what a great fish he is and what will he bring in the market if the flesh is good. He took the bait like a male and he pulls like a male and his fight has no panic in it. I wonder if he has any plans or if he is just as desperate as I am?

Thoughts of the experience as being simply that normally shared by hunter and hunted are still evident, as the old man reflects on the market value of his catch, but there is a new element. As happens increasingly, Santiago also thinks of the marlin as a creature with intelligence and will.

The development is increasingly clear as the novel unfolds. The fish and he, Santiago reflects, are "Beyond all people in the world." They are "joined together" and there is "no one to help either one of us." Later, he resolves to stay with the fish until death, but adds, "He'll stay with me too, I suppose." When the sun rises further, Santiago expresses the bond between the fish and himself even more strongly: "I love you and respect you very much." When the fish lurches, the old man affirms the unity of their suffering: "You're feeling it now, fish . . . and so, God knows, am I." Thus, he is able to express a desire which is strange for a hunter: "I wish I could feed the fish . . . He is my brother." When the marlin rises from the ocean, the implications of the contest become clearer. It is no ordinary fish. The old man had seen many great fish, but this was "the biggest fish that he had ever seen and bigger than he had ever heard of." From this moment on, the contest is more than ordinary. Santiago signals the change by his impatience with his cramped left hand. He is irritated with his hand, not because it robs him of strength, but because such an impairment is unworthy of the battle. Further, that battle is interpreted as a demand upon Santiago to prove his manhood: "I wish I could show him what sort of man I am." The climax of this stage of development in the relationship is reached when Santiago dismisses thoughts of the commercial value of the marlin and affirms the noble nature of his adversary: "There is no one worthy of eating him from the manner of his behavior and his great dignity."

From that moment on, the man and the fish draw closer. They are one in spirit. They are one in conflict, the conflict that noble wills must wage as their preordained task in the universe. Thus, at times, the result of the contest is unimportant:

> You are killing me, fish, the old man thought. But you have a right to. Never have I seen a greater, or more beautiful, or a calmer or more noble thing than you, brother. Come on and kill me. I do not care who kills who.

Consequently, the moment of death is full of pathos and emphasizes the bond between hunter and hunted:

> . . . I want to see him, he thought, and to touch and to feel him. He is my fortune, he thought. But that is not why I wish to feel him. I think I felt his heart, he thought.

After death, the communion of man and fish is not relaxed. The old man does not tow the fish; they are sailing together. When the first shark strikes, Santiago's feelings are explicitly expressed: "When the fish had been hit it was as though he himself were hit." The killing of the fish, the old man reflects, was a demand made by the nature of existence. Perhaps the act was a sin. That he cannot fully comprehend. All he knows is that between the fish and himself there was the bond that unites all creation—the hunter and the hunted, the pursuer and the pursued, the aggressor and the victim:

> Besides, he thought, everything kills everything else in some way. Fishing kills me exactly as it keeps me alive. The boy keeps me alive, he thought. I must not deceive myself too much.

Faced with such inevitability, all creatures can do no more than summon the dignity and nobility of their strength and fulfil their appointed tasks with truth. Thus, when the marlin is mutilated and consumed, everything has been spoiled. Its death and defilement become Santiago's own crucifixion:

> "*Ay*," he said aloud. There is no translation for this word and perhaps it is just a noise such as a man might make, involuntarily, feeling the nail go through his hands and into the wood.

The process of development is clear. In the struggle with the marlin, Santiago has become united with the fish. The fish, then, is more than a fish; its significance goes far beyond the physical. It has become an image of identification. On the ocean, Santiago has entered into the realm of metaphysical things by his identity with his prey. Through their bond as creatures, he has gained insight into the mysteries of the universe. The universe, he sees, preordains its creatures to appointed tasks which they must accept. Faced with the task, the creature can only exercise the nobility of its inner resources. Sad though the truth may be, it must be accepted.

Santiago's only fault lay, not in killing the marlin, but in venturing too far out. He had penetrated regions forbidden to man. He had learned truth which is not ordinarily revealed to man. Like Conrad's Kurtz (*The Heart of Darkness*), he had gained forbidden knowledge. This concept underlines the symbolic nature of the sea in the story. The sea is a common symbol for life and the mysteries of life, and quests for meaning are often expressed in terms of voyages. Melville's *Moby Dick* is a striking example of this quest imagery. Thus, shaken by the mysteries of his bad luck, Santiago had thrown off normal constraints and ventured out into the spiritual depths, farther than other fishermen dared to sail. His quest had been successful. He returned undefeated to battle once more. But he was beaten on this occasion, for a man who ventured too far out could not go unpunished.

Given this interpretation, it may well be that the sharks which beat Santiago themselves become an image. They might be thought of as the ancient force of Nemesis—the inevitable, destructive fate of the man who dares to know what God knows and who dares to act as God acts. In so daring, man exhibits what the Greeks called *hubris*, an arrogance not rightfully his. God is God, and man is man. Confronted by this fact, man is not permitted all knowledge, for that belongs to God alone. When man aspires to know more than the universe allows, he is in a state of *hubris*. In this condition, retribution is inevitable. Fate, or nemesis, will vent its corrective fury upon man. The sharks do no less to Santiago.

The old man is aware of what he has done, and he is equally aware of the penalty:

"Half fish," he said. "Fish that you were. I am sorry that I went out too far. I ruined us both."

Themes

In a sense, *The Old Man and the Sea* is capsulated Hemingway. That is, in its poetic brevity it is the distilled essence of the writer's most profound beliefs concerning human existence. Therefore, to understand the attitudes implicit in that book, it is necessary to bear in mind other works written by Hemingway. They—to use a Hemingway metaphor—are the seven-eighths of the iceberg which remains hidden in *The Old Man and the Sea*.

The basis of Hemingway's position lies in that approach to life called existentialism. It has been observed, with much truth, that there are as many kinds of existentialism as there are existentialists. However, a common fundamental concept in existentialism is that of the Void or Nothingness. Man's life is conceived as a mystery unconnected with any absolutes outside himself. There is, for example, no figure of God as Father watching wisely over the activities of His children, and there is no Heavenly Kingdom awaiting the soul which dies. Death is the one great Absolute. All other propositions of absolutes—society, nation, law, morality, philosophy, theology—are simply pretences which man offers to cover and hide his apprehension of the Void. Man—that is, all human beings—is alone in a universe which is, at best, indifferent to his struggle to live. In this situation, man is thrown back upon his own resources, and particularly upon the resources of his own spirit and intelligence. What he is is all that is precious and real. He must be himself, for being himself he will express his true humanity.

The explanation which is offered here is, of course, dangerously brief and dogmatic. There are, for example, many existentialists who would criticize what has been written. However, the main features of what has been presented can be held to be a reliable explanation. Certainly, they help us to understand the Hemingway posture as we see it in his works.

In 1933, Ernest Hemingway published a short story with the title "A Clean, Well-Lighted Place." As with many of his stories, the plot is relatively simple. There are three main characters—an old man, a middle-aged waiter, and a young waiter. The old man, lonely and melancholy, frequently visits late at night the café where the waiters work. He drinks too much and he stays late. His presence irritates the young waiter, who wants to close the café and return as quickly as possible to his wife and home. The middle-aged waiter is much less fretful than the young man. He is unhurried because he is more responsive to the needs of others who might enter the café late at night seeking solace in their loneliness. Thus, he says, "Each night I am reluctant to close up because there may be some one who needs the café." This, the younger waiter cannot comprehend, because there is much about life that he has not yet comprehended. The older waiter knows the truth, and he expresses it in a parody of the Lord's Prayer which communicates all the existentialist's vision of *nada*, or nothing:

> . . . What did he fear? It was not fear or dread. It was a nothing that he knew too well. It was all a nothing and a man was nothing too. It was only that and light was all it needed and a certain cleanness and order. Some lived in it and never felt it but he knew it was all nada y pues nada y pues nada. Our nada who art in nada, nada be thy name thy kingdom nada thy will be nada in nada as it is in nada. Give us this nada our daily nada and nada us our nada as we nada our nadas and nada us not into nada but deliver us from nada; pues nada. Hail nothing full of nothing, nothing is with thee.

The insight was not new to Hemingway in 1933. Four years earlier, *A Farewell to Arms* had been published. Towards the close of that book, the central figure, Frederick Henry, having fled from the senseless brutality of the war in Italy, waits while the woman he loves, Catherine, is giving birth to their child. The baby is born dead, and Frederick is filled with foreboding about Catherine's fate. In his reflections, he pictures life in terms of two metaphors. The first is that of life as a cruel game:

> . . . Now Catherine would die. That was what you did. You died. You did not know what it was about. You never had time to learn. They threw you in and told you the rules and the first time they caught you off base they killed you.

The second metaphor is in the form of a parable suggested by an earlier experience:

> Once in camp I put a log on top of the fire and it was full of ants. As it commenced to burn, the ants swarmed out and went first towards the centre where the fire was; then turned back and ran towards the end. When there were enough on the end they fell off into the fire. Some got out, their bodies burnt and flattened, and went off not knowing where they were going. But most of them went toward the fire and then back toward the end and swarmed on the cool end and finally fell off into the fire. I remember thinking at the time that it was the end of the world and a splendid chance to be a messiah and lift the log off the fire and throw it out where the ants could get off onto the ground. But I did not do anything

but throw a tin cup of water on the log, so that I would have the cup empty to put whiskey in before I added water to it. I think the cup of water on the burning log only steamed the ants.

The metaphors are vivid and intense. They present a haunting picture of the universe without "rules." If there is a God, then, like Frederick Henry, he is a capricious being. Life and death are simply expressions of the impulse of the moment. There is no beneficent plan for human beings, only incomprehensible and unpredictable ironies and ambiguities.

This point of view can be discerned as a background in *The Old Man and the Sea*, and helps in the identification of the novel's themes.

Probably the most common and clearest interpretation of *The Old Man and the Sea* sees the book as an allegory of man's struggle with life. Thus, Santiago is all men who confront the universe. The fisherman becomes representative man through the parallels drawn between himself and Christ. Like Christ, he has both conviction and humility. Also like Christ, he suffers alone for his faith. The faith of Santiago is, of course, far from orthodox religious faith. It includes his pride in his vocation and his resolve to kill the fish and his determination to show what a man can endure. Like Christ, Santiago suffers; he too has torn hands and a back which knows pain. Yet neither is defeated. Both are, in a sense, beaten: Christ is crucified, and Santiago loses his great marlin. But even as Christ experienced the resurrection, so, we are confident, Santiago will rise once more to meet the future, for the boy will join him again and bring him luck. Finally, also like Christ, Santiago, while being representative man in grappling with life's mysteries alone and enduring alone, is exceptional man. His heart may respond to the wild fancies of creation, as his sympathy for the creatures of the ocean shows, but he is—profoundly and defiantly—"a strange old man." Not for him is the safety of the deep wells of water near the shore; not for him is the companionship of the usual fishing grounds. He ventures further than others, and he vanquishes a fish bigger than anyone has seen or heard of. He is, then, exceptional man, the venturer who dares more than others, testing the limits of human experience. Further elaboration on the parallel with Christ can be found elsewhere (see IMAGERY). The parallel is an important aspect in the interpretation of the novel as an allegory of the human experience and must not be overlooked.

However, the story is not a Christian allegory. The Christian view of the universe is founded upon the proposition of the existence of God, whose benevolent purposes are supreme. No such purposes govern the universe of Santiago. His world is a mysterious, ambiguous mixture of violence and peace, of cruelty and nobility, of death and benevolence. The sea, as both *el mar* and *la mar* is the image of this ambiguity. The same irony pervades the fisherman's relationship with the marlin. He loves and respects it; it is his brother. But he will kill it. For that is the nature of life:

> . . . everything kills everything else in some way. Fishing kills me exactly as it keeps me alive.

The ironic tension inherent in existence is clearly expressed by the old man after his first struggle with a shark: "I killed the shark that hit my fish."

In such a world, the problem facing the old man is an existential problem. His response is in accordance with the Hemingway hero's code of conduct. In this situation, all a man can do is to prove his manhood, to demonstrate all that it means to be human. The task is never completed. The proof is demanded in every experience, as Santiago observes:

> . . . But I will show him what a man can do and what a man endures.
>
> "I told the boy I was a strange old man," he said. "Now is when I must prove it."
>
> The thousand times that he had proved it meant nothing. Now he was proving it again. Each time was a new time and he never thought about the past when he was doing it.

That Santiago succeeds gloriously in his self-appointed task is plain. He endures with fortitude. He suffers triumphantly. And, in the end, he faces the future. The fault he has committed is no sin. It has been the fault of one who has dared too much; he went out too far. He sought a battle which tested his manhood to the limit and, in so doing, he brought misfortune upon himself and the great fish. But the lasting impression is one of the splendor of the old man's daring, and not of the folly of his endeavor.

Thus, in his allegory, Hemingway has displayed for all to see the glory that is man. Proud and courageous, resolute and defiant, accepting and enduring, man is shown to have resources that are equal to the demands made by the universe. This vision is what prompts Burhans' poetic statement of Hemingway's achievement in *The Old Man and the Sea*:

> Through perfectly realized symbolism and irony, then, Hemingway has beautifully and movingly spun out of an old fisherman's great trial just such a pragmatic ethic and its basis in an essentially tragic vision of man; and in this reaffirmation of man's most cherished values and their reaffirmation in the terms of our time rests the deepest and the endur-

ing significance of *The Old Man and the Sea*. ("Hemingway's Tragic Vision of Man" in *Ernest Hemingway: Critiques of Four Major Novels*, edited by Carlos Baker, p. 155)

The novel has also been interpreted as allegory in a different direction. The interpretation here sees the book as a parable of Hemingway's own struggle with his art. Hemingway's previous book, *Across the River and into the Trees*, had not met with critical success. That book, in Stewart Sanderson's words, "was probably more important to its author than to his public," for in it Hemingway "failed to accommodate in a consistent and satisfying way the literal level of his story and the symbolic levels at which he was working also." Thus, the next book, *The Old Man and the Sea*, was crucial for the writer in his career. Magnificently, what had failed in the last work succeeded splendidly in the next, for in that work, Sanderson declares, "Hemingway has never written more universally or meaningfully of himself than in this most externalized of all his stories; like Santiago determining to justify his reputation as a skilled fisherman." This parallel between Santiago and Hemingway has been expressed most succinctly by Philip Young:

> . . . *The Old Man and the Sea* is, from one angle, an account of Hemingway's personal struggle, grim resolute and eternal, to write his best. With his seriousness, his precision and his perfectionism, Hemingway saw his craft exactly as Santiago sees his. The fishing and the fishermen turn out to be metaphors so apt that they need almost no translation: Santiago is a master who sets his lines with more care than his colleagues, but he has no luck any more. It would be better to be lucky, he thinks, but he will be skillfully exact instead; then when the luck comes he will be ready for it. Once he was very strong. "The Champion" they called him, and he had beaten many rivals in fair fights. The boy agrees: "There are many good fishermen and some great ones. But there is only you." Still there are many who do not know this, and the whole reputation is gravely imperilled by a streak of bad luck. And so the ex-champion musters his confidence: "I may not be as strong as I think . . . But I know many tricks and I have resolution."("*The Old Man and the Sea*: Vision and Revision," in *Twentieth Century Interpretations of The Old Man and the Sea*, edited by Katharine T. Jobes, p. 21)

The interpretation is beguiling and attractive, and it may possess some element of truth. However, it does tend to make the novel a very private parable which would be lost on the ordinary reader. Moreover, it seems to complicate interpretation too much, for it demands recognition of the novel, first, as a parable of human existence and then, second, it demands the interpretation of *that* parable as a further parable. That process hardly seems typical of Hemingway's method.

Finally, an important theme in *The Old Man and the Sea* is its affirmation of the bond uniting all creation. That bond is not the expression of empty sentimentality. Artists of every generation have perceived it as belonging to the deepest reaches of truth. In an obvious way, our contemporary concern over environmental issues is the result of a growing apprehension of that bond. Thus, the universe, it is realized increasingly, is not simply man's treasure chest, a gift of God to be exploited and used as man sees fit. The temptation to view the universe in these terms has traditionally been strong. A misreading of religious texts has led to a concept of man as the supreme creature in creation, destined to exercise a sovereign lordship over all others. Just 'a little lower than the angels,' man has succumbed to the temptation to act arrogantly and thoughtlessly and insensitively. Writers and artists, on the other hand, have seen the *malaise* clearly, and have affirmed the reality of the bond of creatureliness uniting all things.

This, for example, is the experience of D.H. Lawrence in his poem, *Snake*. A snake visits his well to drink, and the poet, trained by society and tradition to regard the snake as hostile, chases the snake from the garden. However, he questions his action and laments it. If there were an intruder, he sees, then that intruder was himself, an insight which is emphasized by his being dressed in pyjamas, the garments that symbolize the way in which man has covered his natural self with the heavy disguises of sophistication and civilization.

Similarly, Theodore Roethke, in *A Field of Light*, declares that until man meaningfully apprehends his bond with all things, he is a blind creature, unable to respond to the world around him. Before man experiences this vision he possesses a "twisted" eye; afterwards, he is able to comprehend the beauty of all things and "move with the morning."

In poetry, the clearest statement of the need for and importance of this insight is found in Coleridge's *Rime of the Ancient Mariner*. Like Santiago, the mariner undertakes a fateful voyage. In the beginning, he is arrogantly and egotistically man. In a moment of egotistical caprice, he shoots an albatross which has been following the ship. Disaster follows fast. The favorable winds die, and the ship is becalmed on a burning, tropical ocean. The message is clear: man, in the person of the mariner, has demonstrated the disjunction between himself and the universe. It is only when the mariner, alone and close to death, gives thanks for life spontaneously and selflessly that deliverance comes. Ironically, he praises life that would normally seem loathsome and repulsive—the writhing water snakes that coil and uncoil on the steaming ocean. The lesson is all the more sharply realized for that irony. The insight is clear: man is one with all creatures.

The moral is not trivial. It shapes and fashions man's approach to the universe and dictates his stance in the world. Thus, Santiago sees it as an aspect of the human tragedy. The creatures of the world are like man. They inhabit the same universe, and they must engage in the same struggle. The small, tired warbler that visits the skiff and the magnificent marlin that struggles so gloriously really share the same struggle for existence. And that struggle is Santiago's also. All that he can do is to fulfil his appointed task. Born a fisherman, he must accept his role and hunt his prey. If he does it well, he will prove what a man is.

Thus, there is no egotism or arrogance in Santiago's actions. His pride is simply the confidence he has in his artistry. But his chief response is one of humble love and respect for his ocean brothers. The novel is thus a moving expression of that tragic kinship which unites all creation. The words of Carlos Baker provide a fitting conclusion:

> To their hazard or their sorrow, Hemingway's heroes sometimes lose touch with nature. Jake Barnes in the Parisian café-circle and Fred Henry in the toils of war on the plains of Italy are two memorable examples. Their health ordinarily returns when they re-ally themselves with the natural laws and forces which wait unchanged for the errants' return. But Santiago is never out of touch. The line which ties him to the fish is like a charged wire which guarantees that the circuit will remain unbroken. Saint Francis with his animals and birds is not more closely allied to God's creation than this Santiago with his birds and his fish. These are his brothers, in all the sizes . . . he is convinced of what he has only momentarily forgotten: no man is ever alone on the sea. This sense of solidarity with the visible universe and the natural creation is another of the factors which help to sustain him through his own long ordeal. ("Hemingway's Ancient Mariner," in *Ernest Hemingway: Critiques of Four Major Novels,* edited by Carlos Baker, p. 163)

*The Heroic Impulse

Most of Hemingway's novels emphasize what men cannot do, and define the world's limitations, cruelties, or built-in evil. *The Old Man and the Sea* is remarkable for its stress on what men can do and on the world as an arena where heroic deeds are possible. The universe inhabited by Santiago, the old Cuban fisherman, is not free of tragedy and pain but these are transcended, and the affirming tone is in sharp

*Editor's title. From *The Old Man and the Sea,* by Leo Gurko, *College English,* Vol. 17, No. 1 (October, 1955).

contrast with the pessimism permeating such books as *The Sun Also Rises* and *A Farewell to Arms.*

One aspect of this universe, familiar from the earlier works, is its changelessness. The round of Nature—which includes human nature—is not only eternal but eternally the same. The sun not only rises, it rises always, and sets and rises again without change of rhythm. The relationship of Nature to man proceeds through basic patterns that never vary. Therefore, despite the fact that a story by Hemingway is always full of action, the action takes place inside a world that is fundamentally static.

Moreover, its processes are purely secular in character: Hemingway's figures are often religious but their religion is peripheral rather than central to their lives. In *The Old Man and the Sea,* Santiago, the principal figure, is a primitive Cuban, at once religious and superstitious. Yet neither his religion nor his superstitious beliefs are relevant to his tragic experience with the great marlin; they do not create it or in any way control its meaning. The fisherman himself, knowing what it is all about, relies on his own resources and not on God (in whom he devoutly believes, just as Jake Barnes, while calling himself a bad Catholic, is also a devout believer). If he succeeds in catching the fish, he "will say ten Our Fathers and ten Hail Marys . . . and make a pilgrimage to the Virgen de Cobre" (*The Old Man and the Sea,* Scribner's, 1952, p. 71), but these are rituals that come after the event and have no significant relationship with it.

In this universe, changeless and bare of divinity, everyone has his fixed role to play. Santiago's role is to pursue the great marlin, "That which I was born for" (p. 44), he reflects; the marlin's is to live in the deepest parts of the sea and escape the pursuit of man. The two of them struggle with each other to the death, but without animosity or hatred. On the contrary, the old man feels a deep affection and admiration for the fish. He admires its great strength as it pulls his skiff out to sea, and becomes conscious of its nobility as the two grow closer and closer together, in spirit as well as space, during their long interlude on the Gulf Stream. In the final struggle between them, his hands bleeding, his body racked with fatigue and pain, the old man reflects in his exhaustion:

> You are killing me, fish. . . . But you have a right to. Never have I seen a greater, or more beautiful, or a calmer or a more noble thing than you, brother. Come on and kill me. I do not care who kills who. (p. 102)

On the homeward journey, with the marlin tied to the boat and already under attack from sharks, Santiago establishes his final relationship with the fish, that great phenomenon of Nature:

You did not kill the fish only to keep alive and to sell for food, he thought. You killed him for pride and because you are a fisherman. You loved him when he was alive and you loved him after. If you love him, it is not a sin to kill him. (p. 116)

A sense of brotherhood and love, in a world in which everyone is killing or being killed, binds together the creatures of Nature, establishes between them a unit and an emotion which transcends the destructive pattern in which they are caught. In the eternal round, each living thing, man and animal, acts out its destiny according to the drives of its species, and in the process becomes a part of the profound harmony of the natural universe. This harmony, taking into account the hard facts of pursuit, violence, and death but reaching a stage of feeling beyond them, is a primary aspect of Hemingway's view of the world. Even the sharks have their place. They are largely scavengers, but the strongest and most powerful among them, the great Mako shark which makes its way out of the deep part of the sea, shares the grandeur of the marlin. Santiago kills him but feels identified with him as well:

But you enjoyed killing the *dentuso*, he thought. He lives on the live fish as you do. He is not a scavenger nor just a moving appetite as some sharks are. He is beautiful and noble and knows no fear of anything. (pp. 116-117)

Nature not only has its own harmony and integration but also its degrees of value. In *The Old Man and the Sea* this is contained in the idea of depth. The deeper the sea the more valuable the creatures living there and the more intense the experience deriving from it. On the day that he catches the great marlin, the old man goes much farther out than the other fishermen and casts bait in much deeper water. The marlin itself is a denizen of the profounder depths. Even the Mako shark lives in the deep water and its speed, power, and directness are qualities associated with depth. There are, in fact, two orders in every species: the great marlins and the lesser, the great sharks and the smaller, bad-smelling, purely scavenger sharks who dwell in shallower water and attack with a sly indirectness in demeaning contrast with the bold approach of the Mako. There are also two kinds of men—as there have always been in Hemingway—the greater men and the lesser, heroes and ordinary humans.

To be a hero means to dare more than other men, to expose oneself to greater dangers, and therefore more greatly to risk the possibilities of defeat and death. On the eighty-fifth day after catching his last fish, Santiago rows far beyond the customary fishing grounds; as he drops his lines into water of unplumbed depth he sees the other fishermen, looking very small, strung out in a line far inland between himself and the shore. Because he is out so far, he catches the great fish. But because the fish is so powerful, it pulls his skiff even farther out—so far from shore that they cannot get back in time to prevent the marlin being chewed to pieces by the sharks. "I shouldn't have gone out so far, fish," he said. "Neither for you nor for me. I'm sorry, fish" (p. 121). The greatness of the experience and the inevitability of the loss are bound up together. Nature provides us with boundless opportunities for the great experience if we have it in us to respond. The experience carries with it its heavy tragic price. No matter. It is worth it. When Santiago at last returns with the marlin still lashed to the skiff but eaten away to the skeleton, he staggers uphill to his hut groaning under the weight of the mast. He falls asleep exhausted and dreams of the African lions he had seen in his younger days at sea. The next morning the other fishermen gaze in awe at the size of the skeleton, measure it to see by how much it is record-breaking, while the reverential feeling of the boy, Manolin, for the fisherman is strongly reinforced. Everyone has somehow been uplifted by the experience. Even on the lowest, most ignorant level, it creates a sensation. The tourists in the last scene of the story mistake the marlin for a shark but they too are struck by a sense of the extraordinary.

The world not only contains the possibilities of heroic adventure and emotion to which everyone, on whatever level, can respond, but it also has continuity. Santiago is very old and has not much time left. But he has been training Manolin to pick up where he leaves off. The boy has been removed by his parents from the old man's boat because of his bad luck, but this in no way diminishes the boy's eagerness to be like Santiago. The master-pupil relationship between them suggests that the heroic impulse is part of a traditional process handed down from one generation to another, that the world is a continuous skein of possibility and affirmation. This affirming note, subdued in Hemingway's earlier fiction, is sounded here with unambiguous and unrestricted clarity.

Indeed, Santiago is the clearest representation of the hero because he is the only major character in Hemingway who has not been permanently wounded or disillusioned. His heroic side is suggested throughout. Once, in Casablanca, he defeated a huge Negro from Cienfuegos at the hand game and was referred to thereafter as *El Campéon*. Now in his old age, he is hero-worshipped by Manolin who wants always to fish with him, or, when he cannot, at least to help him even with his most menial chores. At sea Santiago, sharing the Cuban craze for baseball, thinks frequently of Joe DiMaggio, the greatest ballplayer of his generation, and wonders whether DiMaggio, suffering from a bone spur in his heel, ever endured the pain which the marlin is now subjecting him to. And at night, when he sleeps, he dreams of lions playing on the beaches of Africa. The constant association with the king of ball-players and the king of beasts adds to the old man's heroic proportions. He is heroic even in his bad luck. The story opens with the announcement that he has gone eighty-four days without taking a fish—ordinary men are seldom afflicted with disaster so outsized.

Heightening and intensifying these already magnified effects is the extraordinary beauty of Nature which cozens and bemuses us with its sensuous intoxications. The account of the sea coming to life at dawn is one of the most moving passages in the story, supplemented later at rhapsodic intervals by the drama of the great pursuit. This comes to its visual climax with the first great jump of the marlin when, for the first time, Santiago sees the gigantic size of his prey. Hemingway pays very close attention to the rippling and fluting of the water, to wind currents, the movements of turtles, fish, and birds, the rising of sun and stars. One is filled not simply with a sense of Nature's vastness, but of her enchantment. This enchantment adds an aesthetic dimension to Santiago's adventure, an adventure whose heroism invests it with moral meaning and whose invocation of comradeship and identity supply it with emotional grandeur.

Within this universe, where there is no limit to the depth of experience, learning how to function is of the greatest importance. It is not enough to have will; one must also have technique. If will is what enables one to live, technique is what enables one to live successfully. Santiago is not a journeyman fisherman, but a superb craftsman who knows his business thoroughly and always practises it with great skill. He keeps his lines straight where others allow them to drift with the current. "It is better to be lucky," he thinks. "But I would rather be exact. Then when luck comes you are ready" (p. 36). To be ready—with all one's professional as well as psychological resources—that is the imperative. One reason that Hemingway's stories are so crammed with technical details about fishing, hunting, bull-fighting, boxing, and war—so much so that they often read like manuals on these subjects—is his belief that professional technique is the quickest and surest way of understanding the physical processes of Nature, of getting into the thing itself. Men should study the world in which they are born as the most serious of all subjects; they can live in it only as they succeed in handling themselves with skill. Life is more than an endurance contest. It is also an art, with rules, rituals, and methods that, once learned, lead on to mastery.

Furthermore, when the great trial comes, one must be alone. The pressure and the agony cannot be shared or sloughed off on others, but must be endured alone. Santiago, his hands chafed and bleeding from the pull of the marlin, his face cut, in a state of virtual prostration from his struggle, several times wishes the boy were with him to ease the strain, but it is essential that he go unaccompanied, that in the end he rely on his own resources and endure his trial unaided. At the bottom of this necessity for solitariness, there is the incurable reliance on the individual which makes Hemingway the great contemporary inheritor of the romantic tradition. The stripping-down of existence to the struggle between individual man and the natural world, during the course of which he rises to the highest levels of himself, has an early echo in Keats's line "Then on the shore of the wide world I stand alone. . . ." In modern fiction it is Melville and Conrad who give this theme its most significant shape. The mysterious, inscrutable, dramatic Nature into which their heroes plunge themselves in search of their own self-realization supplies Hemingway with the scaffolding for *The Old Man and the Sea*. Like Captain Ahab, like Lord Jim, Santiago is pitched into the dangerous ocean; for only there, and with only himself to fall back on, can he work out his destiny and come to final terms with life.

The concept of the hero whose triumph consists of stretching his own powers to their absolute limits regardless of the physical results gives *The Old Man and the Sea* a special place among its author's works. It confronts us with a man who is not only capable of making the ultimate effort, but makes it successfully and continuously. This theme of affirmation, that had begun to be struck in *Across the River and into the Trees*, is presented here much more convincingly. Colonel Cantwell of the immediately preceding novel is forever talking about his heroism; Santiago acts his out. Cantwell reminisces on past triumphs; the old fisherman demonstrates them before our eyes. The strain of boastful exhibitionism that causes some readers to regard Hemingway as an adolescent Byron spoiled Cantwell's story. It is almost totally absent from Santiago's.

Here we have entered a world which has to some degree recovered from the gaping wounds that made it so frightening a place in the early stories. The world which injured Jake Barnes so cruelly, pointlessly deprived Lieutenant Henry of his one love, destroyed Harry Morgan at the height of his powers, and robbed Robert Jordan of his political idealism has now begun to regain its balance. It is no longer the bleak trap within which man is doomed to struggle, suffer, and die as bravely as he can, but a meaningful, integrated structure that challenges our resources, holds forth rich emotional rewards for those who live in it daringly and boldly though continuing to exact heavy payment from them in direct proportion to how far they reach out. There is no less tragedy than before, but this has lost its bleakness and accidentality, and become purposive. It is this sense of purposiveness that makes its first appearance in Hemingway's philosophy, and sets off *The Old Man and the Sea* from his other fiction.

After the first World War the traditional hero disappeared from Western literature, to be replaced in one form or another by Kafka's Mr. K. Hemingway's protagonists, from Nick Adams on, were hemmed in like Mr. K. by a bewildering cosmos which held them in a tight vise. The huge complicated mushrooming of politics, society, and the factory age began to smother freedom of action on the individual's part. In his own life Hemingway tended to avoid the industrialized countries including his own, and was drawn from the start to the primitive places of Spain, Africa, and Cuba. For there, the ancient struggle and harmony between man and Nature still existed, and the heroic possibilities so attractive to Hemingway's temperament had freer play. At last, in the drama of Santiago, a drama entirely outside the framework of modern society and its institutions, he was able to bring these possibilities to their first full fruition, and re-discover, in however specialized a context, the hero lost in the twentieth century.

Thus *The Old Man and the Sea* is the culmination of Hemingway's long search for disengagement from the social world and total entry into the natural. This emerges in clearer focus than ever before as one of the major themes in his career both as writer and man. Jake and Bill are happy only in the remote countryside outside Burguete, away from the machinery of postwar Europe. It is when Lieutenant Henry signs his separate peace, deserts from the Italian army, and retires with his love to the high Swiss mountains far removed from the man-made butchery of the war that he enjoys his brief moment of unclouded bliss. The defeated writer in "The Snows of Kilimanjaro," as he lies dying, laments his inability to free himself from the complicated temptations of money, fashion, the life of sophisticated dilettantism, and thinks of his lost talent as resting unspoiled on the remote virginal snows cresting the summit of an African mountain (height on land is plainly the moral equivalent in Hemingway to depth in the sea). Robert Jordan must first disengage himself from the political machinery of Spain before the act of sacrificing his life for his comrades can acquire its note of pure spiritual exaltation.

The movement to get out of society and its artifices is not motivated by the desire to escape but by the desire for liberation. Hemingway seeks to immerse himself totally in Nature not to "evade his responsibilities" but to free his moral and emotional self. Since life in society is necessarily stunting and artificial, cowardice consists not of breaking out of it but of continuing in it. To be true to oneself makes a return to the lost world of Nature categorically imperative. And that lost world, as *The Old Man and the Sea* reveals, has its own responsibilities, disciplines, moralities, and all-embracing meaning quite the equivalent of anything present in society and of much greater value because it makes possible a total response to the demands upon the self. Santiago is the first of the main figures in Hemingway who is not an American, and who is altogether free of the entanglements of modern life. It is toward the creation of such a figure that Hemingway has been moving, however obscurely, from the beginning. His ability to get inside this type of character without the fatal self-consciousness that mars so much literary "primitivism" is a measure of how far he has succeeded, in imagination at least, in freeing himself from the familiar restraints of convention. . . .

*Ernest Hemingway's Religion of Man

In recent years, critics have become increasingly suspicious that it is necessary to read Ernest Hemingway's work on the symbolic as well as on the story level in order to gain a full appreciation of its art. Since the publication of *The Old Man and the Sea*, the suspicion has become first an awareness, then a certainty. Of all Hemingway's work, this one demands most to be read on both levels; and the story, its details, its method of presentation, are sufficiently similar to the balance of his work as to suggest strongly the possibility of a similar reading and perhaps a similar interpretation.

The Old Man and the Sea is, as story, very good Hemingway. It is swiftly and smoothly told; the conflict is resolved into a struggle between a man and a force which he scarcely comprehends, but which he knows that he must continue to strive against, though knowing too that the struggle must end in defeat. The defeat is only apparent, however, for, as in "The Undefeated," it becomes increasingly clear throughout the story that it is not victory or defeat that matters but the struggle itself. Furthermore, *The Old Man and the Sea,* while reasserting the set of values, the philosophy which permeates all of Hemingway, is built upon the great abstractions—love and truth and honor and loyalty and pride and humility—and again speaks of the proper method of attaining and retaining these virtues, and of the spiritual satisfaction inevitably bestowed upon their holder.

The Christian religious symbols running through the story, which are so closely interwoven with the story in fact as to suggest an allegorical intention on Hemingway's part, are so obvious as to require little more than a listing of them here. The Old Man is a fisherman, and he is also a teacher, one who has taught the boy not only how to fish—that is, how to make a living—but how to behave as well, giving him the pride and humility necessary to a good life. During the trials with the great fish and with the sharks his hands pain him terribly, his back is lashed by the line, he gets an eyepiercing headache, and his chest constricts and he spits blood. He hooks the fish at noon, and at noon of the third day he kills it by driving his harpoon into its heart. As he sees the second and third sharks attacking, the Old Man calls aloud "'Ay'" and Hemingway comments: "There is no translation for this word and perhaps it is just such a noise as a man might make, involuntarily, feeling the nail go through his hand and into the wood."[1] On landing, the Old Man shoulders his mast and goes upward from the

*By Joseph Waldmeir, from *PMASAL*, XLII (1956).

sea toward his hut; he is forced to rest several times on his journey up the hill, and when he reaches the hut he lies on the bed "with his arms out straight and the palms of his hands up."[2]

The Christian symbolism so evident here shifts from man to fish—a legitimate symbol for Christ since the beginning of Christianity, as it was a legitimate religious symbol before Christianity—and back to man throughout the story. . . .

Along with the Christ symbols, reinforcing them, but depending on them for its importance, is a rather intricate numerology. It is not formalized—neither is the numerology of Christianity—but it is carefully set forth.

Three, seven, and forty are key numbers in the Old and New Testaments, and in the religion, and Hemingway makes a judicious use of them. The Old Man, as the story opens, has fished alone for forty-four famine days and with the boy for forty more. The Old Man's trial with the great fish lasts exactly three days; the fish is landed on the seventh attempt; seven sharks are killed; and, although Christ fell only three times under the Cross, whereas the Old Man has to rest from the weight of the mast seven times, there is a consistency in the equal importance of the numbers themselves.

But, once it has been established that *The Old Man and the Sea* may be read on the symbolic as well as on the story level, a new problem presents itself, a problem which grows out of the nature of the symbolic level and out of the disturbing realization that the two levels exist harmoniously in the work. I think that the problem may best be expressed by two questions which the discerning reader must have asked himself as he put *The Old Man and the Sea* down: Is the story, as it appears at first glance to be, a Christian allegory? Has the old master tough guy decided, in the words of Colonel Cantwell, "to run as a Christian"? If neither of these questions can be answered with an unqualified affirmative—and I submit that they cannot—then a further question must be asked: Just what is the book's message?

The answer assumes a third level on which *The Old Man and the Sea* must be read—as a sort of allegorical commentary by the author on all his previous work, by means of which it may be established that the religious overtones of *The Old Man and the Sea* are not peculiar to that book among Hemingway's works, and that Hemingway has finally taken the decisive step in elevating what might be called his philosophy of Manhood to the level of a religion.

Two aspects of the total work, including *The Old Man and the Sea,* must be considered at this point in order to clarify the above conclusion on the one hand, and to answer the questions concerning Hemingway's Christianity on the other.

The first of these aspects is Hemingway's concern with man as man, with man in his relation to things of this world almost exclusively. The other world, God, does not often enter into the thoughts, plans, or emotions of a Hemingway character. God exists—most of the characters are willing to admit His existence, or at least, unwilling to deny it—but not as an immanent Being, not ever benevolent or malevolent.

God is sometimes prayed to by the Hemingway hero at moments of crisis, but His aid or succor are never depended upon, never really expected. Thus we have Jake Barnes in the Cathedral at Pamplona, on the eve of his great trial, praying for everybody he can think of, for good bullfights and good fishing; and as he becomes aware of himself kneeling, head bent, he

> was a little ashamed, and regretted that I was such a rotten
> Catholic, but realized that there was nothing I could do about
> it, at least for awhile, and maybe never, but that anyway it
> was a grand religion, and I only wished I felt religious and
> maybe I would the next time. . . .[3]

And thus, too, we have the Old Man, who, after twenty-four hours of his monumental struggle have passed, prays for heavenly assistance mechanically, automatically, thinking, "I am not religious," and "Hail Marys are easier to say than Our Fathers." And after forty-five hours, he says:

> "Now that I have him coming so beautifully, God help me to
> endure. I'll say a hundred Our Fathers and a hundred Hail
> Marys. But I cannot say them now."
> Consider them said, he thought, I'll say them later.[4]

But when the struggle is ended and the full ironic impact of his "victory" is clear, he asks himself what it was that beat him, and answers, "Nothing . . . I went out too far."[5]

He who depends too heavily on prayer, or for that matter on any external aids when faced with a crisis, is not very admirable to Hemingway. In *Death in the Afternoon,* when he wants to describe the unmanliness of a "cowardly bullfighter" girding himself for action, Hemingway places him in church

> in his bullfighting clothes to pray before the fight, sweating
> under the armpits, praying that the bull will embiste, that is,
> charge frankly and follow the cloth well; oh blessed Virgin
> that thou wilt give me a bull that will embiste well, blessed
> Virgin, give me that bull, blessed Virgin, that I should touch
> this bull in Madrid to-day on a day without wind; promising
> something of value or a pilgrimage, praying for luck,
> frightened sick. . . . .[6]

A man must depend upon himself alone in order to assert his manhood, and the assertion of his manhood, in the face of insuperable obstacles, is the complete end and justification of his existence for a Hemingway hero. The Old Man *must* endure his useless struggle with the sharks; Manuel, in "The Undefeated," *must*, in spite of his broken wrist and a terrible goring, go in on the bull six times and accept the horn at last; Jake *must* continue to live as "well" and "truly" and "honestly" as he is able in spite of his overwhelming frustration. And each must face his struggle alone, with no recourse to otherworldly help, for only as solitary individuals can they assert their manhood.

And significantly they must go it alone without regard to otherworldly blame. As far as sin is concerned, Jake would probably say along with the Old Man, "Do not think about sin. It is much too late for that and there are people who are paid to do it. Let them think about it."[7] And Manuel would probably nod agreement.

However, in spite of such obvious rejections of otherworldly Christianity in his affirmation of Manhood, Hemingway has formulated as rigid a set of rules for living and for the attainment of Manhood as can be found in any religion. These rules, along with the detailed procedure for their application, constitute the second aspect of Hemingway's total work to be considered in this paper.

The rules are built upon the great abstractions mentioned above. They are so bound up with the procedure for their application that the procedure itself might be considered to be a rule—or better, that neither rules nor procedure exist without one another. Hemingway's philosophy of Manhood is a philosophy of action; a man is honest when he acts honestly, he is humble when he acts humbly, he loves when he is loving or being loved. Thus, taking an awareness of the rules as he has taken an awareness of the abstractions for granted, Hemingway concerns himself primarily with the presentation of procedure. The procedure is carefully outlined; it is meticulously detailed. If no part of it is overlooked or sloughed off, it must result in a satisfying experience almost in and of itself.

This procedure, this ritual—for such is what the procedure actually amounts to—is most clearly evident in Hemingway's treatment of the bullfight. *Death in the Afternoon* is devoted to an evaluation of the manhood of various bullfighters on the basis of their ability to abide by the rules, and to a description of the ritual by means of which they prove possession and communicate the satisfaction to be gained from a proper performance of function to the spectator. War, the prize ring, fishing, hunting, and making love are some of the other celebrations by means of which Hemingway's religio-philosophy of Man is conveyed. But the bullfight is the greatest because, besides possessing, as the others do also, a procedure inviolate, intimately related to the great abstractions, it always ends in death. It assumes the stature of a religious sacrifice by means of which a man can place himself in harmony with the universe, can satisfy the spiritual as well as the physical side of his nature, can atone for the grievous omissions and commissions of his past, can purify and elevate himself in much the same way that he can in any sacrificial religion. The difference between Hemingway's religion of man and formal religion is simply—yet profoundly—that in the former the elevation does not extend beyond the limits of this world, and in the latter, Christianity for example, the ultimate elevation is totally otherworldly.

The bullfighter is in a sense a priest, performing the sacrifice for the sake of the spectator as well as for his own sake, giving each that "feeling of life and death and mortality and immortality" which Hemingway described in *Death in the Afternoon,* and, as does the Roman Catholic priest on the ideal level, the bullfighter actually places his own life in jeopardy. This curious phenomenon of the sacrificer gambling on becoming the sacrificed serves to clarify the terms of Hemingway's system, rather than, as at first glance it might seem, to confuse them. The bullfighter recognizes the possibility and immanence of death when he steps into the ring, and he must face it bravely. He must perform the sacrifice cleanly, with one true stroke, preserving both his honor and the bull's dignity. If he kills out of malice or out of fear his actions will show it, and the spectator will be distracted from concentration upon the sacrifice to awareness of the man, and no satisfaction will result.

There must be a cognizance of death both from the standpoint of killing and from that of being killed; there must be more than a cognizance actually; there must be an acceptance. Knowledge of death's inevitability so that he does not react to its immediacy, coupled with unconcern for the possibilities of life after death, are necessary attributes of the ideal bullfighter. His aim can extend no further than the great abstractions themselves, how he earns them and how he communicates them. He must realize that it is not *that* one dies but *how* one dies that is important. And equally important, that it is not *that* one kills but *how* one kills.

It is not only in his treatment of the bullfight that this second aspect of Hemingway's total work is evident, though there it may be most immediately apparent. The abstractions, the rules, the ritual, the sacrifice dominate the details of *The Old Man and the Sea* as they dominate those of "The Undefeated" and *The Sun Also Rises.* We are told carefully, painstakingly, how the Old Man performs his function as fisherman; how he prepares for the hoped-for struggle:

> Before it was really light he had his baits out and was drifting with the current. One bait was down forty fathoms. The second was at seventy-five and the third and fourth were down in the blue water at one hundred and one hundred and twenty-five fathoms. Each bait hung head down with the

shank of the hook inside the bait fish, tied and sewed solid and all the projecting part of the hook, the curve and the point, was covered with fresh sardines. Each sardine was hooked through both eyes so that they made a half-garland on the projecting steel.

. . . Each line, as thick around as a big pencil, was looped onto a green-sapped stick so that any pull or touch on the bait would make the stick dip and each line had two forty-fathom coils which could be made fast to the other spare coils so that, if it were necessary, a fish could take out over three hundred fathoms of line.[8]

We are told how he hooks the fish and secures the line, waiting suspensefully for the fish to turn and swallow the bait, then waiting again until it has eaten it well, then striking, "with all the strength of his arms and the pivoted weight of his body," three times, setting the hook; then placing the line across his back and shoulders so that there will be something to give when the fish lunges, and the line will not break. We are told specifically, in terms reminiscent of such descriptions of the bullfight, how the kill is made:

The old man dropped the line and put his foot on it and lifted the harpoon as high as he could and drove it down with all his strength, and more strength he had just summoned, into the fish's side just behind the great chest fin that rose high in the air to the altitude of a man's chest. He felt the iron go in and he leaned on it and drove it further and then pushed all his weight after it.[9]

The immanence of death for the sacrificer as well as for the sacrificed, and his total disregard of its possibility, are made clear at the climax of the struggle when the Old Man thinks: "You are killing me, fish. . . Come on and kill me. I do not care who kills who."[10]

It is at this point I think that the questions asked earlier in this paper can be answered. Has Hemingway decided to "run as a Christian"? I think not; the evidence in *The Old Man and the Sea,* with the exception of the Christian symbolism, indicates that he is no more Christian now than he was when he wrote *The Sun Also Rises.* But the Christian symbolism *is* in the book, and it *does* appear to constitute a Christian religious allegory. Yes, but on a superficial level. The religious allegory, attached to the two aspects of the total body of Hemingway's work as they appear in *The Old Man and the Sea*, which have been the subject of most of my discussion thus far, actually constitute a third level on which *The Old Man and the Sea* must be read—as the allegorical interpretation of the total body of the work.

I said above that Hemingway is no more Christian now than he was thirty years ago; it has been my intention in this paper to show that he was *no less religious* thirty years ago than he is now. The evidence which I have presented adds up to something more than a philosophy or an ethic, the two terms which have most often been used to describe Hemingway's world view; it adds up to what I would call a Religion of Man. Hemingway did not turn religious to write *The Old Man and the Sea*. He has always been religious, though his religion is not of the orthodox, organized variety. He celebrates, he has always celebrated, the Religion of Man; *The Old Man and the Sea* merely celebrates it more forcefully and convincingly than any previous Hemingway work. It is the final step in the celebration. It is the book which, on the one hand, elevates the philosophy to a religion by the use of allegory, and on the other, by being an allegory of the total body of his work, enables us to see that work finally from the point of view of religion.

1 Ernest Hemingway, *The Old Man and the Sea* (New York: Scribner, 1952), p 118.

2 *Ibid.*, p. 134.

3 Hemingway, *The Sun Also Rises* (New York: Scribner, 1926), pp. 99-100.

4 *The Old Man and the Sea*, p. 96.

5 *Ibid.*, p. 133.

6 Hemingway, *Death in the Afternoon* (New York: Scribner, 1932), p. 90.

7 *The Old Man and the Sea*, p. 116. Hemingway has always had a deep respect for Christians—provided they *live* like Christians. His great abstractions are also great Christian virtues; and when he finds a believer, such as the priest in *A Farewell to Arms* or Anselmo in *For Whom the Bell Tolls,* who lives in accord with the abstractions, he praises him as "a Christian," and adds, for the benefit of the hypocritical, "something very rare in Catholic countries."
    There is no evidence of intentional blasphemy in any of his work; the deeply religious are frequently exalted, not in the terms of Christianity, but in Hemingway's own terms. In the one-act play, "Today is Friday," Christ's Manhood is given far greater importance than His Godhead with no blasphemous overtones. The First Soldier, speaking for Hemingway and offering the highest praise he is capable of, answers, "He was pretty good in there today," each time the cynical Second Soldier minimizes Christ's manliness. The words are not only directly addressed to the cynic, but indirectly to the emotionally disturbed Third Soldier as well, who has had a religious experience which the First cannot share, but which he comprehends and sympathizes with.

8 *The Old Man and the Sea*, pp. 33-34.

9 *Ibid.*, pp. 103-104.

10 *Ibid.*, p. 102.

Review of Criticism

On *The Old Man and the Sea*

As might be expected, a number of prominent critics have written on *The Old Man and the Sea*. What follows is a brief synopsis of the commentaries of some of the major critics.

Clinton S. Burhans

In his essay, *"The Old Man and the Sea*: Hemingway's Tragic Vision of Man,"* Mr. Burhans contends that the central expression of *The Old Man and the Sea* is the relationship between individualism and interdependence. Man must, through the agony of "isolated individualism," learn of "solidarity and interdependence," and this must be learned in a universe that "dooms such individualism." This, to Burhans, is Hemingway's view of the tragic irony of man's fate.

Burhans also sees in *The Old Man and the Sea* Hemingway's reaffirmation of man's most cherished values: courage, love, humility, solidarity, interdependence.

Carlos Baker

Mr. Baker, in his book, *Hemingway*, writes that *The Old Man and the Sea* revolves around the epic individualism of Santiago. The critic sees the work as a Christian allegory with the old fisherman, of course, representing Christ.

Robert P. Weeks

Robert P. Weeks in his "Hemingway and the Uses of Isolation" shares Gurko's view that *The Old Man and the Sea* reflects Hemingway's desire for liberation from involvement in the social world in order that he might escape to the isolation of the natural world. Weeks writes, "from the first eight words of *The Old Man and the Sea* . . . we are squarely confronted with a world in which man's isolation is the most insistent truth."

This, of course, is in contrast to the views of Mr. Burhans, who maintains that Hemingway was affirming man's interdependence as well as his individualism.

Philip Young

Philip Young devotes a section of his book, *Hemingway,* to *The Old Man and the Sea* in which he points to the epic stature of the novel.

He notes that Hemingway is concerned with life: the unconquerable natural forces against which a man struggles only to lose in the face of impossible odds. The loss is death, but a man can dominate this loss with dignity and thus achieve a victory. The novel is an "epic metaphor," and Mr. Young likens it to a contest in which the problem of moral right and wrong seems petty and unimportant in the face of the monumental struggle of life.

Keiichi Harada

Mr. Harada in his article, "The Marlin and the Shark," explores the symbolism of *The Old Man and the Sea*. He expounds the thesis that the novel is a satisfying work of art because Hemingway recognizes the "multi-layeredness" of literature as a basis of a "good" and "true" work of art. Mr. Harada provides a convincing discussion of the following symbolical images: old man and the ocean, lions and the bone spur, and marlin and the shark.

On Ernest Hemingway's Works as a Whole

The stream of Hemingway criticism has been continuous and enormous, and gives no signs of drying up. Scholarly publications such as *College English, Modern Fiction Studies, American Literature, English Journal, Criticism, Fitzgerald-Hemingway Annual* continue to publish serious essays on Hemingway. Critics in virtually every country have examined his work. Such international critical attention is perhaps even more significant than the Nobel Prize awarded to Hemingway in 1954. That Ernest Hemingway is one of the major figures in American literature is indicated by the fact that in sheer bulk there is more writing about his work than the author himself ever produced.

Foreign Critics

This is not to say that critical opinion on Ernest Hemingway is unanimous, although there has been greater agreement on *The Old Man and the Sea* than there has been on either *For Whom the Bell Tolls* or *Across the River and Into the Trees*. Foreign critics have tended to be enthusiastic about Hemingway's work, but have viewed it in broadly cultural rather than in strictly aesthetic terms, seeing in his writing a reflection of the violence that is so close to the surface of the American character.

With the exception of a few critics such as Arturo Barea, who insist that Hemingway was trapped by his own preoccupations even—or especially—when dealing with other cultures, there seems among foreign critics to be a certain fascination with Hemingway the man rather than with Hemingway the artist; and the result has tended to be sociological and psychological comment about him rather than literary analysis.

Hemingway and His Critics

English and American critics have not been altogether free from the enchantment of the "Hemingway image." From the very beginning, much critical ammunition has been expended on Hemingway's personal life and personal philosophy, rather than upon the art for which this philosophy provided the raw material. Hemingway was often impatient, to put it mildly, with those "schoolmarm" critics who insisted on rapping his knuckles for moral reasons instead of looking at his books as books. In 1929, for example, when Hemingway was already being hailed—and denounced—as spokesman for the Lost Generation, he wrote a "Valentine" to his critics:

Sing a song of critics
pockets full of lye

four and twenty critics
hope that you will die
hope that you will peter out
hope that you will fail
so they can be the first one
be the first to hail
any happy weakening or sign of quick decay.
(All very much alike, weariness too great,
sordid small catastrophes, stack the cards on fate,
very vulgar people, annals of the callous,
dope fiends, soldiers, prostitutes,
men without a gallus . . .)

(From Little Review 12, May, 1929, p. 42)

There may be some justification for seeing the scavenger sharks—*los Galanos*—as those critics whom Hemingway viewed throughout his career as literary scavengers feeding on the hope of weakening or decay in the artist.

Adverse Criticism

Not all the adverse criticism, however, has been the work of "schoolmarm" critics. From Sean O'Faolain to Leon Edel, from Wyndham Lewis to Harry Levin, critics and creative writers have attacked what they view as extremely "thin" art, an art whose protagonists could deal with complexity only by running away from it. "Think of nothing," says Santiago the fisherman, and this is a slogan not only for the old man, but for virtually every Hemingway hero. The Hemingway protagonist takes refuge in what can be interpreted as mindless action—action in which killing men is put on the same level as shooting animals, and shooting animals is put on the same level as making love to women, and making love to women is put on the same level as drinking wine.

Hemingway's art, in the phrase of the prominent scholar, Leon Edel, is an art of evasion rather than of confrontation; anything that the Hemingway hero could not reduce to a sort of extension of his own ego, Edel and other critics insisted, was simply eliminated from any consideration whatsoever, and the result was an art based less on true economy of style than of failure of imagination. According to this view, by eliminating all that could not fit into his private ritual, Hemingway produced books of the mindless for the mindless, books which (despite a certain narrative skill and ease in reading) reduced human motivations to an adolescent formula, and human love to an autoerotic image.

If the Hemingway woman was, as Edmund Wilson once remarked, "amoeba-like," the Hemingway man was hardly more impressive—except, of course, when shooting something, or hitting something, or catching something, or drinking something, or being hit by something, or making love. That Joe DiMaggio is held up as a symbol of heroism in *The Old Man and the Sea* is significant. The fact that in his very last novel Ernest Hemingway used a big-league baseball player to represent human glory is perhaps a comment on his vision both as a man and as an artist. Perhaps one might sum up the anti-Hemingway school of criticism in the following phrase: "He was the best seventeen-year-old novelist who ever lived."

Favorable Criticism

Those critics who see Hemingway as a major artist, however—and their number is legion—insist that Hemingway's work is simple only on the surface; that his heroes are neither callous nor mindless, but possessed of enormous sensitivity both to human dishonesty and universal suffering; that his style communicates far more than it overtly states; and that in his best books Ernest Hemingway is a lyric poet of the English language. Such critics—among them Carlos Baker, and Philip Young—remind us that for Ernest Hemingway, the real world is an arena where the human soul must struggle to face its own mortality. If he did limit his subject matter, they insist, he did so deliberately, in order to achieve an essentially formal and symbolic, rather than realistic, art.

That Hemingway is capable of complete realism is indicated by those scenes that he chooses to render with breathtaking precision. That he has deliberately limited his subject matter to particular types and situations is hardly unique with Hemingway. From workers in stone such as the Greek sculptors, to workers in words such as the American novelist, Henry James, creative artists have always limited their subject matter, and have so utilized it that the subject transcends its limitations.

The subject or material that an artist uses is less important than is the universality he achieves. In this respect, as Carlos Baker has pointed out, Hemingway is perhaps the United States' most universal writer. His work has been translated in all parts of the world, and speaks to the essential humanity of individual human beings of all cultures and all races.

The Stature of Hemingway

Ernest Hemingway may well have been more sophisticated than most of his critics. He read widely, and was deeply aware of literary development and history. He distrusted overembellishment, and insisted (as he remarked in *Death in the Afternoon*) that the age of the baroque is over. Such a conviction is as legitimate as any other for the working artist, who, after all, must develop his own style and his own craft so that they will serve as an instrument for his particular vision of human destiny. The Hemingway vision was shaped by the horror and chaos of World War I, a war that marked the end of the baroque, and that symbolized the empty rhetoric of Western culture.

The Hemingway vision, despite the violence of his subject matter, is an affirmative one. In a period when annihilation hangs like a sword of Damocles over the world, Hemingway offers resources of human strength, and the hope for individual value. His "code," as Mark Spilka has pointed out, "gives meaning to a world where love and religion are defunct, and where the proofs of manhood are difficult and scarce and where every man must learn to define his own moral conditions and live up to them."

Whether for praise or blame, Hemingway critics have agreed upon one thing: he is one of the great figures of our time. Almost a legend in his own lifetime, Hemingway was a remarkable man as well as a remarkable writer.

Review Questions and Answers

Question 1.
Discuss the aesthetic design of *The Old Man and the Sea*.

Answer
The Old Man and the Sea has a clearly discernible rhythm. It starts off on a soft note. We are introduced to Santiago and follow the quiet strains of his daily life as revealed in the dialogue between the old fisherman and his devoted young friend, Manolin. We get the impression that this first act, as it were, is a prelude to more crucial events that lie ahead. The tone is one of quiet anticipation of the events to come on the following day. The preparations in the black of night for the fishing trip retain the foregoing calm qualities.

At dawn, on the gulf stream, a small pulse-beat of action is felt in the endless life-death struggle for survival of the sea creatures. The presence of Santiago is a moving force behind the quickening of the tempo. Excitement mounts as a big fish nibbles at the bait. A climax is reached in the strike of the marlin. The feeling of agitation is sustained in the drive for the open sea and in the peril of the situation. Although the agitation abates, the tension is maintained while Santiago reflects on his spiritual kinship with the fish, which stems from his basic respect for all life. On the third day, a radiant note of success and joy is sounded as Santiago wins his battle with the fish. Tragedy almost immediately follows. At first, Santiago fights back in the clash between good and evil, but eventually he resigns himself to his loss. The tone then changes from somberness and painful struggle to serene acceptance and spiritual triumph.

The drama comes full circle as Santiago docks. The tone at the end is not tragic but triumphant; the dignity of man has prevailed.

The design of the whole is carefully wrought. Hemingway deftly modulates tone and changes tempo and makes compelling the triumph spawned from the seeds of defeat and despair. Hemingway's accomplishment here is remarkable, for, in enabling Santiago to prevail he has remained free of sentimentality and artificial contrivance.

Question 2.
Examine the relationship between Santiago and the marlin.

Answer
Santiago pities the great fish and feels that they are bound together in brotherhood. Although Santiago respects the marlin, he vows to kill him before the end of the day. In the midst of the struggle, the old man pauses to reflect, and endows the fish with his own qualities: nobility, calmness and endurance. The marlin, like Santiago, has a tremendous will to live and bolsters this will with stamina as though he had conserved his strength for this preordained moment. At first, Santiago believes the great fish is being treated unjustly but then finds justification in the realization that his actions demonstrate what a man can do and endure. He acknowledges that the marlin's right to attempt to kill the man is as inviolable as the man's right to attempt to kill the marlin. In his reflections, Santiago continually thinks of the great fish as his friend and his brother.

Question 3.
In what way does Santiago relate to other Hemingway heroes?

Answer
Despite the fact that Santiago is an old man, with the days of his strength and youth behind him, he shares many characteristics with other Hemingway heroes—characteristics that for Hemingway were essential aspects of heroism. There is the trinity of values that Hemingway admired all his life: will, pride and endurance. These three qualities enable a man to maintain his initiative, to shape action according to his own will, to set up a ritual of life—and death—and so provide a framework of form about a chaotic universe.

Manhood was for Hemingway a matter of this initiative, an ability (through willed endurance) to set up a code or ritual of action. All of Hemingway's heroes are heroic in their ability to control, to endure. In this respect, Santiago represents a continuation of, rather than a departure from, the Hemingway code.

Santiago, furthermore, is—like other Hemingway protagonists—unwilling, and perhaps unable, to pursue ultimate metaphysical or intellectual problems. When Santiago asks himself whether he has the right to kill the marlin, or even the noble Mako shark, his only answer is that such questions are too difficult to manage, and that he must concentrate on the work, the action, or the killing. In this sense, Santiago represents the Hemingway retreat no less than the Hemingway code; for the code represents a retreat from all complexities, to those areas in which action can be justified on its own terms, and in which the justification for action need not be examined at all.

Santiago differs from a protagonist like Robert Jordan (in *For Whom the Bell Tolls*) chiefly in his refusal to rely upon social or political sloganeering to justify the action, or the killing, in which he is involved. Both in his virtues (will, pride, endurance) and in his limitations (an avoidance of all complexity and reduction of human motivation to self-contained action and ritual) Santiago remains very much a hero cut to the pattern that Hemingway followed throughout his career.

Question 4.

On what basis does Santiago associate himself with the great DiMaggio?

Answer

Santiago sees in Joe DiMaggio, the baseball player, much of his own will, pride and endurance. Like Santiago, DiMaggio (at the time of reference) is no longer the great champion he once was. He suffers, moreover, from much pain because of a bone spur in his heel. DiMaggio, however, continues to "play the game," using his skill, his heart, and his endurance to replace his early strength. In this way, he is as much of a man as he was in his youth, and perhaps even more so, since it is the qualities of will rather than mere strength that make a champion. This is why Santiago associates himself so closely with the ballplayer (whose father, incidentally, was a fisherman).

Question 5.

Hemingway had often expressed his dread of old age and the loss of initiative and will (the loss of manhood). Give a brief comment on how Hemingway in *The Old Man and the Sea* resolved this dilemma of old age.

Answer

In the last decade or so of his life, Hemingway was searching for a posture that would enable him to cope with the grim reality of his own age. Hemingway's temporary, but vivid, solution was a change of personal role: he would dramatize what he could not avoid.

If the early Hemingway had been an almost legendary figure of youthful and virile adventure, the older Hemingway would take up the role of Grand Old Man, the battle-scarred veteran, the aging but still indomitable combatant.

The resources of age rather than the powers of youth would

henceforth be Hemingway's public role, and this was to provide the substance of his literary role as well. *The Old Man and the Sea*, published in 1952, is the story not of youthful disillusion or youthful love in a world of chaos; it is the story of an aged champion for whom the power of will has replaced the power of flesh, and the wisdom of humility and true pride has replaced the arrogance of simple pessimism and romantic self-sacrifice.

Humility and true pride, however, are not qualities likely to be possessed either by the crusading idealist (such as Robert Jordan), or by protagonists of alienation—protagonists who, like Frederick Henry in *A Farewell to Arms*, refuse to play the game of life if the rules are not to their liking.

The qualities of humility and pride must be forged in a man's own soul. Only when the individual neither requires nor uses external crutches, whether of affirmation, nostalgia or negation, can he achieve that power of selfhood (which for Hemingway is synonymous with manhood) that old Santiago the fisherman achieves in his open boat, alone with his pain, his endurance, his love for the noble marlin that is his opponent, his defeat and his ultimate triumph.

This triumph, furthermore, is a victory only in spiritual terms, for it is only in spiritual terms that victory can ever be real. Ultimately, the only "cause" is a man's own being, his own truth. Romantic love is an illusion of youth, the political or social motivation is either so complex as to be meaningless, or so corrupt as to defeat its own rhetorical purpose.

Unlike Robert Jordan, Santiago does not attempt to justify his struggle in terms of externals. Unlike Frederick Henry, he does not attempt to worship a sacred object—a kind of love goddess for whose sake all things may be sacrificed. For Santiago, the only justification for life is living, and the only justification for death is dying. He is a fisherman and the great marlin is a fish, and, joined together by a larger pattern in which each is merely a part, they fulfil their destinies.

Question 6.
Who are the outsiders in *The Old Man and the Sea*?

Answer
In any Hemingway work, the outsiders are those who do not follow the code of will, pride and endurance, or those who—through ignorance or brute appetite—do not understand how mortality (and time) can be redeemed by the code, or ritual-of-action. The tourists, for example, cannot understand the glory of Santiago's struggle. Mere spectators of the struggle of life, they have neither dignity, pride nor the will that alone can redeem man's inevitable defeat. The scavenger sharks, who swallow flesh even as they die, are mere brute mechanisms for feeding, knowing nothing beyond their own digestion.

Question 7.

How does *The Old Man and the Sea* exemplify the Hemingway code?

Answer

The Hemingway code of manhood does not involve mere physical strength, sexual potency or ability to accumulate (or spend) wealth. According to this code, a man is measured by his will, pride and endurance: the endurance to accept pain, even loss when the loss cannot be avoided; the pride of knowing that one has done one's best, with the courage to act truly according to one's own nature; and the will to accept defeat or victory without whining or boasting.

Santiago the fisherman does embody this code, which is essentially one of dignity rather than success. Santiago, despite his old age and poverty, is a man in the fullest sense of the word. Although his strength is gone, his endurance and willed courage permit him to conquer the marlin. Faced with defeat, he does not quit. Knowing that he has no chance against the sharks, for example, he continues the struggle against them. Destruction but not defeat is the quintessence of the Hemingway code.

Question 8.

Discuss *The Old Man and the Sea* as a work of literary symbolism.

Answer

Literary symbolism is a method that organizes the facts of real life and real experience, so that these facts come to have greater meaning than is implied in a literal sense. Symbolic meaning must arise naturally from the facts, rather than be superimposed upon them. Symbolism might be described as "reality-plus"—a way of writing in which the facts echo in the mind with a significance beyond that of the story. In this sense, *The Old Man and the Sea* is a work of literary symbolism.

The story of Santiago is very real indeed. Hemingway writes with his usual care and precision in achieving an exact portrait of "the way it was" in real life; every detail of the fishing is clearly recreated. Over and above this reality—or perhaps one should say permeating it—is an echo of additional meaning. Christian symbolism runs throughout the book: the piercing headache suffered by Santiago, the wounds in his hands, the scene in which he carries the mast up the hill, the way he falls asleep in the position of the Cross and the love and awe with which he is regarded by Manolin, his disciple. The parallel to the suffering and nobility of Jesus is clear enough.

This is not to say that Santiago is necessarily a Christ figure. The crucifixion is itself a symbol of willed sacrifice, of the power and beauty of the human spirit. Other interpretations of *The Old Man and the Sea* are quite possible. Indeed, more than one meaning might be right—and this too is characteristic of literary symbolism.

Some critics have seen the book as symbolizing the pain, suffering, loneliness and glory of the artist who does what every artist must do: attempt to go "too far out." Even the scavenger sharks may be seen as symbolizing those who are governed by appetite, feeding on the artist's agony and endurance.

Still another interpretation may be that *The Old Man and the Sea* is, in essence, a clarification of Hemingway's own attitudes on the inevitability of old age; for in creating the character of Santiago, Hemingway has demonstrated the values that may become stronger rather than weaker with advancing age.

The essential point is that *The Old Man and the Sea* does have these echoes of meaning that transcend the facts of the story, although the facts themselves are beautifully and realistically described.

Question 9.
Why does Manolin insist that Santiago has not been defeated?

Answer
Manolin, the disciple of Santiago, has learned more than fishing from the noble old man. He has learned that the means are always more important than the ends, that the success of one's struggle is of less importance than is the struggle itself. Manolin understands what a heroism of pride, will and endurance the old man's struggle must have involved. To get such a fish, against all odds, in the face of loneliness and pain, is actually far more important than the loss of the marlin to the scavenger sharks. What happened with the sharks could have happened to anyone (sooner or later a similar loss—death itself—must happen to all men). Santiago's duel with the marlin was the work of a true representative of the divine greatness of the human spirit when it is true to its own humanity.

Question 10.
What meaning do you attach to the young lions of Santiago's dream?

Answer
One of the major characteristics of a literary symbol is that no single meaning can be attached or fixed to the symbol. For this reason, it is very difficult to fix one meaning to the symbol of the young lions in Santiago's dream.

As a symbol, the image of the young lions communicates a particular quality of emotion that serves to complement the theme of the novel and the nobility of Santiago. This emotion is one of grandeur, of simplicity, of power without meanness, and of the eternal youth that

Santiago represents. Santiago is young in spirit, if not in flesh, and in the last analysis, this may be the most important youth of all. It is fitting that Santiago should dream of lions rather than of wealth, or violence, or women; the "old man" of Hemingway's novel is eternally young even in his great age.

Question 11.

Discuss the distinguishing characteristics of Hemingway's writing style.

Answer

What strikes us first about Hemingway's style is its remarkable simplicity, both in diction and sentence construction. It is a bare, unadorned style that has lured many writers to imitate it, but only Hemingway has been able to use it with any success. It would appear that anyone could write like Hemingway, which could not be said of James or Joyce or Faulkner, but to have a simple style is not necessarily to write simply. The danger is that when you try to simplify, you end up writing like a child. Hemingway's art is a polished, mastered art no less difficult to effect than that of James or Proust.

Helping to create this air of simplicity is a frequent use of the word, "and." In one paragraph of six sentences and 119 words, "and" appears twelve times.

Hemingway's writing is consistently sensual and concrete. He distrusted abstraction. Critics have accused him of being anti-intellectual and even primitive, but Hemingway would have welcomed this as praise, for his purpose was to communicate life in all its rich materiality.

Hemingway was indeed a master of vivid description. His prose examined the details of clouds, coast, sky and water, giving more than just color and shape. One could almost experience the actual feel and smell of the air and sea. The sequence and choice of words create the motion of the boat on the swells of the sea. The inner eye can see the limitless dimensions of the seascape and the vastness of the horizon. We discover that there is actually no emptiness of ocean as usually imagined, but myriad lives and activities.

Another quality of Hemingway's style, especially evident in *The Old Man and the Sea*, is its lyrical beauty. The novel as a whole could easily be accepted as one of the great poems in the language. It certainly recalls Wordsworth's remarkable poem, *Michael*. Their styles are marked by a similar classical simplicity, and their subject and theme are the same: the inherent dignity of natural man. Both heroes overcome a painful event late in life, thereby asserting their true spiritual worth.

Question 12.

Discuss point of view in *The Old Man and the Sea*.

Answer

Hemingway uses several approaches to tell the story of *The Old Man and the Sea*. The most prominent is straight narrative, with Hemingway, the objective narrator, simply telling what is happening.

Sometimes, however, the author steps aside and we get an opportunity to know the inmost thoughts of Santiago. We are admitted into his mind as he reflects and muses. Consciousness, of course, is more complex, elusive and cryptic than this, but Hemingway was not attempting what Joyce made central in *Ulysses*. Hemingway also has Santiago speak aloud to himself to vary the pattern of the novel.

There is also ordinary dialogue. The point of view here is the one found in drama. The audience directly confronts the characters, with the author, as it were, in the wings. It should be noticed that Hemingway himself is not felt in the book. He nowhere directly injects his own sentiments or attitudes, but rather conveys them implicitly through action and character. The book, in effect, has written itself; it is an autonomous entity.

Suggested Study Topics

1. The novella, or short novel, has had a long and honorable history in American literature, and some critics claim that it is the literary form in which American writers have particularly distinguished themselves. Henry James, Stephen Crane, Willa Cather, F. Scott Fitzgerald, William Faulkner, and Ernest Hemingway are several of the best American novelists who have exploited the shorter form. You might find it worthwhile to make a study of the form and see if you can find reasons for its apparent appeal.

2. In recent studies of American literature, the distinction between the romance and the novel has increasingly occupied the attention of critics. Is it possible that the short novel, or novella, is more congenial to the romantic writer? Why? Is that because the fable and the allegory also tend to partake of the romance? Consider the question specifically in relation to *The Old Man and the Sea*, and see what conclusions you reach about its form.

3. The greatest American romance about the sea is Herman Melville's *Moby Dick*. It too draws upon the tall tale, folklore, fable, and allegory, and it too centers upon the chase for a great fish. It might be interesting to compare it with *The Old Man and the Sea* in both specific and general ways. For example, the Pequod is a whaler, which contains all races of mankind among its crew; Santiago's boat is a small skiff, and he sails alone. Yet both authors are seeking to universalize their stories, each in a different way. Analyse the differences and similarities.

4. There is an important body of literature dealing with the sea—nonfiction as well as fiction. Such works range from Richard Dana's *Two Years Before the Mast* (1840) and Herman Melville's *White Jacket* (1850), to Joshua Slocum's *Sailing Around the World* (1954) and Joseph E. Garland's *Lone Voyager* (1963), which tells the story of Howard Blackburn of Gloucester, Massachusetts. Compare and contrast the struggles of the heroes of these stories against the forces of nature with those of Santiago.

5. Hemingway once wrote, in *The Green Hills of Africa*: "All modern American literature comes from one book by Mark Twain called *Huckleberry Finn*." Can you find any traces of Twain's influence upon *The Old Man and the Sea* in particular, or upon Hemingway's work in general? What do you think Hemingway meant by such a statement?

6. The influence of Hemingway upon contemporary writers has been enormous. In fact, one of his so-called imitators, John O'Hara, once wrote of Hemingway as "the outstanding author since the death of Shakespeare." Can you define what is meant by the Hemingway influence and trace its impact upon other writers as diverse as James M.

Cain, John O'Hara, William Saroyan, Raymond Chandler, andAlfred Hayes? Undoubtedly you can add to the list.

7. The Hemingway code, sometimes referred to as "grace under pressure," and often displayed in violent sports, such as bullfighting, is an interesting subject for further study. Although the Hemingway hero is usually defeated physically, as Edmund Wilson first observed, he appears to win moral victories. Trace the development of the typical Hemingway hero from Hemingway's early short stories to Santiago in *The Old Man and the Sea*.

8. Alfred Kazin has written that Hemingway "brought a major art to a minor vision of life"—a provocative statement indeed. Can you defend it or disprove it? Since Kazin first made the statement in the early 1940's, it may not apply to Hemingway's later novels. What do you think? What might other good critics of Hemingway say of his work? Be as specific as possible.

Bibliography

Barbour, James, and Robert Sattelmeyer, "Baseball and Baseball Talk in 'The Old Man and the Sea'," *Fitzgerald-Hemingway Annual,* 1975.

Baskett, S.S., "The Great Santiago: Opium, Vocation, and Dream in 'The Old Man and the Sea'," *Fitzgerald-Hemingway Annual,* 1976.

Burhans, Clinton S., Jr., "'The Old Man and the Sea': Hemingway's Tragic Vision of Man," *Hemingway and His Critics.*

Colvert, James B., "Ernest Hemingway's Morality in Action," *American Literature* XXVII (November, 1955).

Cooperman, Stanley, "Hemingway and Old Age: Santiago as Priest of Time," *College English* (December, 1965).

D'Agostino, Nemi, "The Later Hemingway," *Hemingway: A Collection of Critical Essays,* ed. Weeks.

Dupee, F.W., "Hemingway Revealed," *Kenyon Review* XV (Winter, 1953).

Fagan, Edward R., "Teaching Enigmas of 'The Old Man and the Sea'," *English Record* VIII (Autumn, 1957).

Frohock, W.M., "Mr. Hemingway's Truly Tragic Bones," *Southern Review* XXXVIII (Winter, 1953).

Handy, William J., "A New Dimension for a Hero: Santiago of 'The Old Man and the Sea'," in Sutherland, W.O.S., Jr., ed., *Six Contemporary Novels.*

Hovey, R.B., "'The Old Man and the Sea': A New Hemingway Hero," *Discourse* IX (Summer, 1966).

Jobes, Katharine T., ed., *Twentieth Century Interpretations of The Old Man and the Sea.* New Jersey, 1968.

Sanderson, Stewart, *Ernest Hemingway.* Edinburgh: Oliver and Boyd Ltd., 1961.

Stephens, Robert O., "Hemingway's Old Man and the Iceberg," *Modern Fiction Studies* VII (Winter, 1961-62).

Sylvester, Bickford, "Hemingway's Extended Vision: 'The Old Man and the Sea'," *PMLA* LXXXI (March, 1966).

Wagner, L.W., "The Poem of Santiago and Manolin," *Modern Fiction Studies* 19 (1973).

Wells, Arvin R., "A Ritual of Transfiguration: 'The Old Man and the Sea'," *University Review* XXX (December, 1963).

Wilson, G.G., Jr., "Incarnation and Redemption in 'The Old Man and the Sea'," *Studies in Short Fiction* 14 (1976).

NOTES

Don't forget to match that tough textbook with helpful

COLES NOTES

Expertly written, fast review summaries designed to give a greater understanding of the subject.

Shakespeare
Antony and Cleopatra
Antony and Cleopatra—Ques. and Ans.
As You Like It
Coriolanus
Hamlet
Hamlet in Everyday English
Hamlet—Ques. and Ans.
Julius Caesar
Julius Caesar in Everyday English
Julius Caesar—Ques. and Ans.
King Henry IV—Part 1
King Henry IV—Part 1
   —Ques. and Ans.
King Henry V
King Lear
King Lear in Everyday English
King Lear—Ques. and Ans.
Macbeth
Macbeth in Everyday English
Macbeth—Ques. and Ans.
Measure for Measure
Merchant of Venice
Merchant of Venice in Everyday English
Merchant of Venice—Ques. and Ans.
Midsummer Night's Dream
Midsummer Night's Dream in
   Everyday English
Midsummer Night's Dream—
   Ques. and Ans.
Much Ado About Nothing
Othello
Othello—Ques. and Ans.
Richard II
Richard III
Romeo and Juliet
Romeo and Juliet in Everyday English
Romeo and Juliet—Ques. and Ans.
Taming of the Shrew
Tempest
Twelfth Night
Winter's Tale

Shakespeare Total
Study Editions
Hamlet
Julius Caesar
King Henry IV—Part 1
King Lear
Macbeth
Measure for Measure
Merchant of Venice
Othello
Romeo and Juliet

Taming of the Shrew
Tempest
Twelfth Night

Reference
Dictionary of Literary Terms
Effective Term Papers and Reports
English Grammar Simplified
Handbook of English Grammar
   and Composition
How to Write Good Essays
   and Critical Reviews
Secrets of Studying English

The Canterbury Tales
Canterbury Tales
Prologue to the Canterbury Tales T.S.E.
Prologue to the Canterbury Tales

French
French Grammar—Ques. and Ans.
French Grammar Simplified
French Verbs Fully Conjugated
French Verbs Simplified

German
German Grammar—Ques. and Ans.
German Grammar Simplified

History
History of Canada
History of the United States

Mathematics
Elementary Algebra Notes
Secondary Sch. Maths 1
Secondary Sch. Maths 4
Senior Algebra Notes

Chemistry
Elementary Chemistry Notes—Revised
How to Solve Chemistry Problems
Introduction to Chemistry
Senior Chemistry Notes—Revised

Physics
Elementary Physics Notes
How to Solve Physics Problems
Senior Physics Notes

Biology
Biology Notes

Philosophy
Philosophy—Ques. and Ans.

Literature / Poetry
Adventures of Huckleberry Finn
Adventures of Tom Sawyer
All Quiet on the Western Front
Animal Farm
Bleak House
Brave New World /
   Brave New World Revisited
Catch 22
Catcher in the Rye, Nine Stories
Chrysalids, Day of the Triffids
Crime and Punishment
Crucible
Cry the Beloved Country
Death of a Salesman
Diviners
Doctor Faustus
Duddy Kravitz and Other Works
Edible Woman
Emma
Fahrenheit 451
Far From the Madding Crowd
Farewell to Arms
Fifth Business
For Whom the Bell Tolls
Frost's Poetry Notes
Glass Menagerie
Grapes of Wrath
Great Expectations
Great Gatsby
Gulliver's Travels
Hard Times
Heart of Darkness
Ibsen's Works
Iliad
Jane Eyre
Joseph Andrews
Keats' Poetry Notes
King Oedipus, Oedipus at Colonus,
   Antigone
Le Morte D'Arthur
Lord of the Flies
Lord of the Rings, Hobbit
Madame Bovary
Man for All Seasons
Mansfield Park
Mayor of Casterbridge
Mill on the Floss
Mrs. Dalloway, To the Lighthouse
Murder in the Cathedral
   & Selected Poems

1984
Odyssey
Of Mice and Men
Old Man and the Sea
Oliver Twist
One Flew Over the Cuckoo's Nest
Paradise Lost
Passage to India
Pearl
Persuasion
Pickwick Papers
Pilgrim's Progress

Portrait of the Artist as a Young Man
Power and the Glory
Pride and Prejudice
Prince-Machiavelli
Pygmalion
Rape of the Lock
Saint Joan
Scarlet Letter
Separate Peace
Sons and Lovers
Stone Angel and Other Works
Stranger, Plague
Streetcar Named Desire
Such is My Beloved, More Joy in Heaven
Sun Also Rises, Snows of Kilimanjaro

Surfacing
Tale of Two Cities
Tess of the D'Ubervilles
To Kill a Mockingbird
Tom Jones
Two Solitudes
Ulysses
Vanity Fair
Waiting for Godot
War and Peace
Who Has Seen the Wind
Wordsworth's Poetry Notes
Works of John Donne
Wuthering Heights
Yeats' Poetry Notes